Waking the Spirit

Waking the Spirit

A MUSICIAN'S JOURNEY HEALING BODY, MIND, AND SOUL

ANDREW SCHULMAN

WITH AN AFTERWORD BY
MARVIN A. McMILLEN, M.D., FACS, MACP

PICADOR
NEW YORK

WAKING THE SPIRIT. Copyright © 2016 by Andrew Schulman. Afterword copyright © 2016 by Marvin A. McMillen. All rights reserved. Printed in the United States of America. For information, address Picador, 175 Fifth Avenue, New York, N.Y. 10010.

picadorusa.com • picadorbookroom.tumblr.com
twitter.com/picadorusa • facebook.com/picadorusa

Picador® is a U.S. registered trademark and is used by St. Martin's Press under license from Pan Books Limited.

For book club information, please visit facebook.com/picadorbookclub or e-mail marketing@picadorusa.com.

Designed by Steven Seighman

Musical arrangement art of Second Lute Suite, BWV 997: Sarabande by Johann Sebastian Bach created by Andrew Schulman.

Library of Congress Cataloging-in-Publication Data

Names: Schulman, Andrew, 1952–
Title: Waking the spirit : a musician's journey healing body, mind, and soul
  / Andrew Schulman ; with an afterword by Marvin A. McMillen, M.D.
Description: First edition. | New York : Picador, 2016. | Includes
  bibliographical references.
Identifiers: LCCN 2015044496 (print) | LCCN 2015045989 (e-book) | ISBN
  9781250055774 (hardcover) | ISBN 9781250055781 (e-book)
Subjects: LCSH: Schulman, Andrew, 1952– | Guitarists—United
  States—Biography. | Music therapists. | Music therapy. | Critical care
  medicine.
Classification: LCC ML419.S326 A3 2016 (print) | LCC ML419.S326
  (e-book) | DDC 780.92—dc23
LC record available at http://lccn.loc.gov/2015044496

Our books may be purchased in bulk for promotional, educational, or business use. Please contact your local bookseller or the Macmillan Corporate and Premium Sales Department at 1-800-221-7945, extension 5442, or by e-mail at MacmillanSpecialMarkets@macmillan.com.

First Edition: August 2016

10 9 8 7 6 5 4 3 2 1

To Peter J. Horoszko (1988–2016)
PJ, whose spirit will always be at the very heart of this book

Author's Note

This is a true story, though some names and details have been changed. No patient referred to in this book has been named or identified without their express written consent.

To the extent that the information contained in this book discusses or involves medical treatments of any kind, it is not intended to replace the advice of the reader's own physician or other medical professionals. In making their own health care decisions, individual readers—or their caretakers—are solely responsible for the results of those decisions, and the author and publisher do not accept responsibility for any adverse effects claimed to result from those decisions.

Contents

Medicina sanat animam per corpus, musica autem corpus per animam.

(Medicine heals the mind, soul, and spirit by the body, but music heals the body by the mind, soul, and spirit.)

—Giovanni Pico della Mirandola, *Conclusiones Nongentae*, 1486

Prologue

I turned the corner into the Surgical Intensive Care Unit and a wave of sound hit me. It always did. Beeps from ventilator machines, infusion pumps, and cardiac monitors. The cacophony of voices of doctors, nurses, patients, and visitors at every volume and intensity. And the ever-present discordance of televisions turned up way too high. It struck me again that this was the worst environment for the critically ill to heal. Today there was another noise, a sound I had never heard before, and I stopped in my tracks, unsure. Strange words, very fast and loud, neither happy nor angry, streamed from a bed at the far end of the hall. A woman's voice talking. But I couldn't understand a word she was saying or even make out the language she was speaking. It was just a barrage of sound. I had no idea what was going on.

The voice flowed out from behind the curtain of Bed 5, taking over the whole ward. I saw nurse Richard Spatafora bolt out and dash to the Nurses' Station, his face anxious. "We need the music therapy tapes. Something. Quickly."

"It's okay," said a nurse. "Andrew's here."

Richard whipped his head toward me. "Thank God," he said. "Andrew, get your guitar ready as fast as you can. We need you." I nodded, pulling my guitar from its case and grabbing my blue music folder marked BACH. I followed Richard behind the curtain, not sure what to expect.

The patient, a woman I guessed to be in her sixties or seventies, sat up in bed with a gauze bandage wrapped around her head. Probably from brain surgery. She looked past me, brilliant blue eyes sparkling, her smile radiant, talking, talking in this loud, melodious tongue. It sounded like Russian. She looked Russian with her high cheekbones. She was beautiful.

There were two other nurses in this small space with Richard, and they all jangled with nerves. Exhausted. Richard shook his head and looked at me. "She's been like this for two hours now." His voice was flat. "She's tied us all up. We can't get her to settle, can't get to the other patients."

I pulled a chair up to the end of the bed, set up my music stand, and for a few moments just looked and listened. The patient was talking still, her monologue seeming never to run dry. What could she be saying? She laughed, looking around, shifting constantly in the bed, fighting to get out. I noticed her arms were restrained, tied to the side rails with white plastic strips. But she didn't seem scared or anxious. I realized she wasn't actually talking to the nurses, but seemed to be conversing with people nearby that only she could see. She smiled the whole time, her words pleading but never angry. It was hard to watch but I couldn't look away. She was so lost, as if she were stuck in another place where we just couldn't reach her.

I settled in, took a deep breath, and started to play my guitar arrangement of the Prelude from Bach's *First Cello Suite*. At the sound of the first note she turned her head toward me, looking at my face and then at my right hand as it plucked the strings of the guitar. Gone was the scattered expression from her face as her eyes gained focus. She stopped talking, her mouth half-open in surprise, silent. Her face and shoulders relaxed, and she smiled. Not the plastered grin of before but a real smile of pleasure. She was here now, in this room, and not wherever she'd been for the past few hours. Something was connecting. We were just ten seconds into the music.

Richard let out a sigh of relief, smiled, and gave me a thumbs-up. I grinned, wide. One by one, Richard and the other nurses left, slipping through the curtain, able to tend to other patients. It was just me and the patient now. The Russian woman.

I played one piece after another for her without a break. She was calm, settled in the bed. Listening. As I brought a chorale melody to an end I paused, thinking about the next piece to play. Immediately, she started to struggle, pulling at her restraints as if she wanted to clamber out of bed. I moved swiftly into a lively Bach minuet—a type of dance. As the music started up, she calmed again. I noticed if I moved my body, swaying to the rhythm of the music, it engaged her attention even more. I decided to spend my whole ninety minutes at her bedside.

She talked to me as I played. I still had no idea what she was saying, but it wasn't the senseless sounds of before. She was communicating with me now. Reaching out, as my music reached out to her. Thirty minutes went by, then an hour, her attention never flagging as long as I was playing. A doctor on rounds stopped by for a minute to check on her. She leaned back when she saw him, looked up, and in a small, childlike voice said, "Beautiful sounds." I was surprised and delighted. She had found her own voice again.

It was almost time for me to leave. I'd been playing short, melodic pieces, and they were working well, keeping the patient calm, but I wanted to go a step further. To play one of Bach's most profound fugues, one of the most intricate forms of music ever devised. I decided on the fugue from the Prelude, Fugue, and Allegro written late in his life. As I started to play the deceptively simple opening melody, she gazed at me, grateful, and settled back into the pillows of her bed. Completely at peace. She closed her eyes, and I played just for her. Somewhere at the edges of my mind I remembered that we were in the Surgical Intensive Care Unit (SICU) and that machines hummed and beeped all around us, but then it was just the music, the patient, and me. For seven minutes I watched her face. The fugue had worked. The word "fugue" comes from the Latin *fuga*, which means "flight" or "fleeing." And the patient had done that. She slept peacefully now, far from this jarring environment, partially healed by music. At the end of the fugue, I packed my guitar and my trusty pages of Bach and slipped away.

I left the SICU that day deep in thought, profoundly affected by the patient in Bed 5. I still thought of her as the Russian woman, although I'd found out from a nurse that she was American, from a small town in upstate New York. The language she'd been speaking at first was gibberish, although a very fluent form of it. I'd learned she had undergone brain surgery the day before and sometimes, after that kind of operation, the nerve synapses misfire for a while and bring on bizarre behaviors. Several things really struck some chords with me. The inability of the nurses, and I knew how great these nurses are, to get through to the patient to help her. The failure of all the modern medicine around her to heal her. The amazing and rapid change that music effected on her, by reaching some deep place in her brain. And the fact that Bach was the agent of that change. I rushed home to my computer, determined to find out everything I could about the power of music to heal. Another leg of my journey had just begun.

I'm now in my sixth year as the resident musician in the SICU at Mount Sinai Beth Israel hospital in New York City. Three times a week I spend ninety minutes there playing my guitar at the bedsides of the critically ill, patients like the woman in Bed 5. Over the years, I've witnessed the most remarkable ways in which music can help the healing process, the ways it can calm a patient or lift their spirits, or reach them when they seem locked in a place that no one else can access. It can soothe a staff member's exhaustion or anxiety and let them refocus on helping a patient, and it can provide a connection for a patient's family, perhaps bring back old memories and open pleasant topics of conversation. I've also seen the beauty that music has brought when nothing could save a patient's life, as it eased the transition from life to death, floating above the sounds of medical machines.

I've been forever changed by my interactions with the patients and medical staff here, by the bridge that music creates between the healthy and the sick. But the event that was most life changing for me was one I didn't witness. Because I was the patient. I was wheeled into this very SICU, clinically dead. A Code Blue. I wasn't expected to live. I was the patient in Bed 11, hooked up to machines and tubes, bloated beyond recognition and surrounded by doctors and nurses. And my wife, Wendy, was the desperate loved one, hoping against hope at my bedside, asking for answers, for a miracle, emotionally raw. Somehow I made it through. I was the sickest person in the SICU back then and music saved my life.

After that I decided to return to the SICU and give back, to use my thirty-five years of experience as a professional musician to bring about positive change in other people's lives. I love it. I love being part of a medical team and being able to say with certainty—and with compelling evidence—that my guitar is both a medical and a musical instrument. There is a clinical research study under way at Mount Sinai Beth Israel on the effects of live music in the SICU, begun in January 2011, exactly a year after I began playing at the hospital, and my music has been part of this study. The study aims to document the effect of live music on the sound environment of the patients, family, and staff and determine whether it has an impact on their level of stress, anxiety, and/or perception of pain, and also—and this is especially interesting—whether it affects the perception of noise in the SICU. I feel very honored to be part of this study.

I've seen countless examples of the power of music to soothe and heal from my position at hundreds of bedsides with my guitar. But why does music have this power? In recent years, there have been numerous studies addressing the impact of music and medicine. The late Dr. Oliver Sacks, formerly a professor of neurology at New York University School of Medicine and world-renowned author, and Mark Jude Tramo, M.D., Ph.D., a professor of neurology and ethnomusicology at UCLA—who founded the world's first Music and the Brain course at Harvard College in 1997—have shed enormous light on the topic. Dr. Sacks in his best-selling book *Musicophilia: Tales of Music and the Brain,* and Dr. Tramo in numerous professional journals including *Science, Journal of Neurophysiology, Journal of Cognitive Neuroscience, Music and Medicine,* and *Contemporary Music Review.*

Dr. Sacks, who along with Dr. Connie Tomaino founded the Institute for Music and Neurologic Function in 1995, has said, "Nothing activates the brain so extensively as music." It goes deeper than that, though. According to John Mondanaro, the clinical director for the Louis and Lucille Armstrong Music Therapy Program at Mount Sinai Beth Israel, the effects of music on the physiological and psychoemotional components of the patient's experience are central to current research efforts.

Compelling results are emerging from an abundance of this new research. Dr. Joanne Loewy, founder and director of the Louis Armstrong Center for Music and Medicine, led a landmark study, published in the journal *Pediatrics* and reported in the *New York Times,* that found that live music is beneficial to vital signs, feeding, and sleep in premature babies, thereby relieving stress and pain. The study also showed that when the babies' parents sang lullabies to them, stress was reduced—in the parents.

In Germany over the last thirty-five years, Dr. Ralph Spintge, president of the International Society for Music in Medicine

(ISMM), with Dr. Loewy, editor in chief of the international journal *Music and Medicine,* has conducted studies analyzing the effects of music on anxiety and pain reduction before, during, and after surgery.

Dr. Kamran Fallahpour, a clinical psychologist, neuroscientist, and director of the Brain Resource Center in New York City, is among a consortium of international neuroscientists who helped develop one of the largest databases in the world of brain, cognitive, and genomic data. As a clinician and researcher he tries to translate the latest neuroscience research findings and technology into clinical practice—including the use of music and sound to help activate or deactivate certain brain areas and regulate the nervous system in order to manage pain, stress, and mood.

Dr. Connie Tomaino has undertaken pioneering research in music therapy with patients suffering from the effects of brain trauma including stroke, Parkinson's, Alzheimer's disease, and other kinds of dementia.

On August 13, 2015, *The Lancet* published a new study that confirmed that listening to music before, during, and after surgery reduces patients' anxiety, pain, and their need for painkillers. The study team, led by Queen Mary University of London, analyzed the results of seventy-three randomized controlled trials that looked at the impact of music on postoperative recovery, and their findings confirmed the positive link between music and lower levels of pain, anxiety, and pain medications. This was true even in cases of surgery performed under general anesthesia. The study concludes, "Music is a noninvasive, safe, and inexpensive intervention that can be delivered easily and successfully in a hospital setting. We believe that sufficient research has been done to show that music should be available to all patients undergoing operative procedures."

These studies—and others like them—provide the scientific underpinning to explain why a guitarist playing for patients in a SICU can have an important and positive role in such key areas as anxiety reduction, pain management, and the prevention of delirium.

Music used for healing is one of the oldest branches in the field of medicine. Early records have been discovered from ancient Egyptian medicine, Babylonian medicine, Ayurvedic (Indian subcontinent) medicine, and classical Chinese medicine that incorporated musical healing. The ancient Greeks valued the relationship between music and medicine in the god Apollo, whose gifts included both the musical and healing arts, and the first use of the term "musical medicine" began with Pythagoras, the fifth-century philosopher-mathematician. The Romans are said to have used musicians in their battlefield hospitals as a form of anesthesia.

Often, as I walk through the halls of the hospital, I see doctors and nurses nod at my guitar and my ID badge and say, "Music, the next big thing in medicine." With the evidence of new research, it just might be. I truly hope so. It would be wonderful to see music being used in hospitals as a cost-effective and noninvasive medical modality, to see hospitals as far better healing environments than, in many cases, they are today. The hospitals that already include music therapy departments understand how important it is to think of what is best for the patients, not just the medical practitioners.

Playing for the patient in Bed 5 was a critical moment for me on a journey that started when I woke up in the SICU. Dr. Marvin McMillen, the director of the SICU when I was a patient and the doctor who first gave permission for me to return as a musician, has said that no one will ever know in medical terms how I survived those first days in my coma, but he's also said that he's sure that music was the turning point in my miraculous recovery. When I first returned to the hospital to play my guitar for other patients I acted intuitively to decide what music to play, for whom, and for how long. But the incredible transition I saw in the so-called Russian woman was a "wow" moment for me that sent me on a quest for knowledge. When I rushed home from the hospital that day and turned on my computer I found this quote, within seconds, from neuromusicologist Dr. Arthur Harvey: "Of all the music we tested in medical school with patients, colleagues and others, Bach's music consistently made the brain work in a balanced way better than any other genre." My brain lit up. I was hooked.

I embarked upon hundreds of conversations with people who shared their experiences and knowledge about music's extraordinary power to heal. Patients and their loved ones, doctors, nurses, music therapists, musicians, professors, authors. And I began to read, to study, to learn.

This abundance of material—from the informal and anecdotal hospital bedside story to cutting-edge scientific research—has helped me understand why a guitarist playing in a SICU can play such a positive role in patient care. It has helped me understand why listening to music enabled the woman with the sparkling blue eyes in Bed 5 to get through the neurological chaos of her postsurgery brain. Music woke her spirit. And in those minutes that I played for her, music helped her as much as any other medicine available to her that day. Maybe more.

If I were not a physicist, I would probably be a musician. I often think in music. I live my daydreams in music. I see my life in terms of music. . . . I cannot tell if I would have done any creative work of importance in music, but I do know that I get most joy in life out of my violin.

—Albert Einstein

1

The Ultimate Reality

THE TELEPHONE RANG.

It was midafternoon, late June 2009. The caller ID showed the name of a doctor I'd seen for the first time a week before. I instantly realized that if my doctor was calling the day after a pancreas scan there was a very good chance I was about to get some very bad news. We'd known for ten months since the first scan revealed two suspicious cysts that things might get serious. I stared at the phone for another second before answering. My wife, Wendy, must have seen my expression. She hurried over, fear in her eyes.

"I just got the results of the scan, and the two cysts from last year are still there but they haven't changed in size, which is a good thing." He paused, and when the next words came his voice had lowered in pitch and darkened in timbre. "But there is something there now that wasn't there ten months ago—a mass the size of a walnut with irregular borders."

Another pause. "Look, I'm going to tell it to you straight. I showed everything to an oncologist who shares my office suite, and I called the radiologist. We all concur—you have pancreatic cancer."

When I'd met with him in his office I'd found his manner off-putting. Now, though, there was a sound of compassion in his voice.

"If it hasn't spread, you may survive this. But the only way to really know what's going on inside is to look with a laparoscope. You need to find a pancreatic surgeon immediately."

"Pancreatic cancer," I said, my voice a whisper. Wendy began to tremble, and I could see she was going to cry. I pulled her in close. Like me, she was a professional musician. She'd barely finished a year of breast cancer treatments—surgery followed by chemo and radiation—and the extra singing she'd been doing to make more money had caused a polyp to grow on her vocal cords. She'd just had another surgery to remove the polyp and was on total vocal rest. She wouldn't be able to talk for another two weeks. There weren't any words to express how we were feeling anyway.

As I listened to the doctor, I wondered if my time might be up. I was fifty-seven years old but I still felt young. At least I did until this moment. Now I felt cold, and numb.

Less than a week later, Wendy and I were sitting in an examination room at Beth Israel waiting for Dr. Martin Karpeh, Jr., the chairman of the hospital's surgery department. When he entered the room we liked him immediately. In his early fifties, handsome, about six feet tall with broad shoulders, he had a quiet charisma and a smile that put us at ease. He exuded professional competence and personal warmth.

We watched him while he read the radiologist's report. When he finished, he looked up and said, "I'm not convinced. I need to look at the pictures. I'll be back in five minutes."

As with many couples that have been together a long time, Wendy and I didn't need to speak. We looked at each other, hoping that maybe this whole thing was nothing more than a terrible nightmare from which we would soon awaken.

Five minutes can seem like an eternity. When Dr. Karpeh finally returned, the ashen expression on his face told me everything. He sat down, looked at me, then Wendy, then back at me, and said, "It's a 98 percent probability of pancreatic cancer. We need to schedule surgery right away." The other doctors had said 100 percent. It was oddly reassuring to get another 2 percent back in my favor.

Over the next fifteen minutes, I learned more than I ever thought I would about pancreatic cancer. I learned that of the approximately forty-nine thousand pancreatic cancer diagnoses every year, 75 percent are discovered too late. There are no symptoms until the cancer has spread to the point when the patient is inoperable and has only months, maybe weeks, to live. I had no symptoms. The 25 percent of cases found early enough to be operable are almost always discovered from a scan that's done while looking for something else, as was the case with me. My father died from a burst aorta, and a year earlier a cardiologist had ordered a CT scan to see if I'd inherited that condition. My aorta was fine; however, that was when the two cysts on my pancreas were seen. Dr. Karpeh explained that as far as he could see in the scans, the cancer had not yet spread. The only way to know with certainty would be through a laparoscopy, the insertion of a thin plastic tube with a tiny video camera attached. He couldn't biopsy—that procedure ran the risk of spreading the cancer. If the laparoscopy showed that the cancer had already spread, he would simply close the incision, and I would be made as comfortable as possible for the short amount of time I had remaining. If there were no signs of cancer beyond the pancreas, then Dr. Karpeh would proceed with surgery and remove the mass.

The last thing I remember from that meeting was that I had a 3.9 percent chance of living another two years. It's hard to be hopeful with those odds. The math told me I had a 96.1 percent chance of joining my ancestors in the near future and during the forty-minute cab ride home that was all I could think of.

A friend who'd been diagnosed with Stage 4 melanoma and survived once told me about Plotinus, a disciple of Plato, who spoke about an "ultimate reality" that transcends the physical world and is beyond all rational knowledge. I lived mostly in this ultimate reality for the two and a half weeks before the operation.

One of the things I remember from that time was a gift of nature. Every day was sunny and mild. It felt like the management upstairs was watching out for me. I shared much of those presurgery days with Dolly, then seven years old, and Paco, five, our furry, four-legged children—two beautiful and exuberant yellow Labrador retrievers. We took long walks every day in Riverside Park along the Hudson River and spent part of each afternoon in the dog run at 105th Street. There was a bench at the south end of the run that I liked in particular. Each day I looked up and saw a rectangular shape formed by the branches of two trees. It seemed to me like a huge TV screen revealing clear blue skies opening up to heaven.

I'd never thought much about heaven, but seeing my own little glimpse of what might be awaiting me, *if* I qualified, calmed me. Over those two weeks, with my dogs settled at my feet, looking through that gateway to the eternal sky above, I was grateful for fifty-seven very good years. At the heart of it was a happy marriage with Wendy, the joy of time spent with our beautiful dogs, and a lifetime in music—playing the guitar—doing what I loved.

Memories came, like home movies. I saw a perfect Sunday morning in August 1960—sunny, breezy, and warm. I was eight years old. We were in the car on the way to the beach, my parents in the front and my two sisters and me in the back. As the car stopped for a red light, my mother turned to me and said, "Your father and I have decided it's time for you to learn to play a musical instrument." It was the Age of Elvis, and an imaginary cartoon bubble with a guitar in it appeared over my head. Though she didn't know it at the time, my mother's dream, that one day I'd be a doctor, vanished into the ether. I became a guitarist in that moment.

A few weeks later, my first guitar teacher, Jane, a tall, blond, leggy nineteen-year-old beatnik, rang our doorbell and my love affair with the guitar began. After nine months, Jane said to my parents, "I've taught him everything I know," and suggested I take classical lessons with Mr. Goldstein, a retired music teacher who lived nearby.

The following week, my father drove me to my first lesson. Hanging on a wall in Mr. Goldstein's house was a photograph of an old man with gray hair, a round face, and thick black-framed eyeglasses, playing a guitar and looking rather stern.

"That's Andrés Segovia, the greatest guitarist of all time," said Mr. Goldstein in a reverent tone.

I nodded. Next to the photograph was a painting of another old man, this one wearing an elaborate white wig and a jacket with silver buttons. He was holding a sheet of music, and had what looked to me like a mischievous smile on his face. I was instantly drawn to him.

"And that's the greatest musician of all time, Johann Sebastian Bach. Sit. Listen." Mr. Goldstein began playing Bach's Little Prelude in D minor. The notes started spinning through the air.

Gazing at that piece of sky, the years flowed by. I saw myself walking out onto the scuffed stage of Carnegie Recital Hall to make my New York concert debut. As I got seated, it seemed to me as if the floorboards looked up and said, "We're not impressed, we've seen it all." I knew I was just one of many who'd sat there. But, oh, how I loved being on that stage.

And Wendy. My mind flashed to our first date. The doorbell rang. There she stood, a petite five foot four with wavy red hair, big blue eyes, a pink sleeveless blouse, and a diffident smile. She walked past me with a nod and took a slow look around the apartment. Clearly unimpressed.

We chatted awkwardly in the kitchen while I made my favorite dinner, garlic spaghetti. I was stoned, and sipping on a big can of Australian beer. I opened another. Halfway through that second can, Wendy fell silent. She gave me a hard look and said,

"You're stoned, and getting drunk, and I'm not comfortable with that." She stalked into the living room, grabbed her bag, and headed for the door. I hurried after her and, turning on the charm, persuaded her to stay, to sit with me on the couch. She started crying so I put my arm around her. To my surprise, she laid her head on my shoulder and confessed she was heartbroken because a guy she liked had broken up with her the day before.

Seven years, and quite a few garlic spaghetti dinners later, we got married.

Two nights before the surgery Dolly jumped up on the bed, circled a few times, and lay down at my feet. I'd always known that the day would come when her life would end and that we would all grieve terribly. Suddenly, it hit me that almost certainly I—her daddy and pack leader—would be leaving *her*. No more joyous reunions every time I came home. She and Paco would wait at that front door for someone who would never walk through it again. I couldn't even explain it to them. I had no way of saying goodbye or thanking them for all they had given to me. I cried for all of us.

Finally, it was the night before the big day. Last-minute packing; time to figure out what to take with me. The two most important items: my iPod, and the choice of a book.

My iPod playlist always varied, but now I filled it with my favorite music. I'd been listening to the *St. Matthew Passion* by Bach a lot in the past two weeks, especially when using the rowing machine in the gym. My favorite piece in the world, and my favorite version of it, recorded in 1962 at Carnegie Hall, conducted by Leonard Bernstein with the New York Philharmonic and great singers, sung not in the original German but in English.

The opening movement—one of the most dramatic pieces of music ever written—begins with the sound of a heartbeat in the basses and a mesmerizing ascending melody played by the flutes and oboes. When the voices of the choir enter, the effect is heavenly. From that point on, the choir and orchestra, actually a double choir and double orchestra, which is part of the enormous power of this music, move to a climax that is both resolute yet pulls forward into an unfolding mystery. You are completely hooked. The first voice that follows, the tenor soloist, the Evangelist, appears suddenly without accompaniment. The contrast to the huge sound of the opening is startling yet so centered and strong. It is riveting. It had got me through to the end of many a rowing session. And, whenever I found myself dwelling on that 3.9 percent chance of living another two years, the *St. Matthew Passion* would lift me to a better place.

I loaded in the other music that I loved: more Bach, the Beatles, Brahms, Ellington, Debussy, Jobim. All the music that moved my heart.

The final choice to be made was, what book to bring? An important decision, as I've been a voracious reader from the same age I started playing the guitar. At the time, I was making my way through Rex Stout's crime series featuring genius detective, Nero Wolfe. My first choice went in the bag, but I reconsidered. The title might have been unsettling to another patient—*Might As Well Be Dead*. I took it out and reached for another that I thought was a better choice:

Not Quite Dead Enough.

Connections between music, religion and healing were very evident in many primitive tribal civilizations in Africa where the shaman (i.e., witch doctor or medicine man) functioned as the tribe's chief musician, medicine man and priest.

The shaman used special songs, rhythms, musical instruments (especially drums, bells and rattles), dances and dramas in conjunction with magic or religious rituals to draw out or drive away illness and disease. Singing was often an indispensable part of the healing process.

—**Jacqueline Schmidt Peters,**
Music Therapy: An Introduction

2

Code Blue

W‍ENDY GLANCED UP once again at the big white clock on the wall of the main waiting room of Beth Israel Medical Center. She was curled up in a chair, her head resting on a pillow, shoes off, and thoroughly exhausted. Her stomach had been in knots all day. Now it was nearly nine P.M., Thursday night, July 16, 2009. I'd been in surgery since two P.M.

Soon after the anesthesiologist put me under, Dr. Karpeh had begun the laparoscopic examination. At around 2:45 P.M., Wendy received a call. The coast was clear. There was no sign the cancer had spread and the operation would proceed. A huge relief, but for the rest of the day, with me still in surgery, Wendy struggled to keep calm.

She heard a sound first before she saw him; someone was walking over to her. Looking up, she saw Dr. Karpeh in purple surgical scrubs and cap, and her first thought was that, although he looked tired, it didn't seem as if he was about to tell her bad news. He wasn't.

He broke into a big smile and said, "You're not going to believe this. The tumor was benign!"

Wendy gets extremely excited when she hears great news. For a split second she almost couldn't believe it, and when she did, she screamed, jumped up, and threw her arms around Karpeh's neck. He looked slightly embarrassed but laughed. He also knew that many of the people sitting nearby were terribly on edge, and so he told Wendy to follow him to one of the small rooms nearby where he could give her a brief report of what had happened.

Wendy's first question was, "How could this be?"

"Every once in a while," Karpeh said, "even when every sign says cancer, it isn't." He explained that the area with the mass in the tail of the pancreas was in necrosis—meaning that it was dying tissue—and showed exactly like malignant mass. That even though the mass was benign, the surgery had been necessary because the necrotic tissue would eventually have destroyed my entire pancreas.

"We still need to do a full pathology test to confirm," he added. "But I'm confident about a good outcome." He grinned and headed toward the door. "Meet me in the SICU. He'll be in Bed 5, all the way at the end of the hall. He'll still be sedated but by the time you get there he'll be coming out of it."

Wendy, deliriously happy, picked up her cell phone and speed dialed my mother, Sylvia. "It's not cancer!" she yelled.

Karpeh, still there, paused briefly to enjoy that moment. Then his beeper went off. Wendy noticed his sudden change of expression.

He looked at her and said with some urgency, "I have to get up there immediately."

She began to follow him. "I'm coming with you."

"Sorry, you can't, you have to take another elevator. Go to the SICU waiting room on the third floor. I'll be with you as soon as I can." He turned and hurried away.

It took her a while to reach the SICU—Beth Israel is a big hospital with many sections and departments, and she got lost several times in the maze. I'm glad she was late to meet me, especially since she didn't go to the waiting room as Karpeh had told her, but instead followed the signs into the SICU itself and rushed past the double doors. What she saw next, as she would say many times afterward, was the most terrifying sight of her life. It would have been even more traumatic had she walked in just a few minutes sooner.

Dr. Mason Mandy, Karpeh's chief resident, had prepared me for the trip to the SICU; the final sentence in my operative report was, "The patient left the OR in stable condition." The report showed that the surgery was perfectly executed. Wheeled on a gurney into the elevator, I was a very lucky postsurgery patient on my way to recovery.

Then, seconds later, I began to do everything I possibly could to die. Inexplicably, my blood pressure started to plummet and my face turned gray. As soon as the elevator doors opened, the race was on.

Under normal circumstances, it's about a five-minute trip to the SICU, but this time it needed to be a lot faster. Dr. Mandy and the anesthesiologist sped me through hospital corridors. Within another minute, my blood pressure was undetectable—and, without it, my heart stopped. I was in cardiac arrest, a term synonymous with clinical death. No heartbeat, no blood circulation, no respiration—a complete cardiovascular collapse. I was a Code Blue, requiring immediate resuscitation.

As we dashed through the double doors into the SICU, Dr. Mandy was pumping my chest, one hundred compressions a minute, in a desperate attempt to preserve my brain function. He saw that Bed 11 right next to the entrance was empty and available, and he directed the gurney transporter to turn hard left. If he'd taken me to my scheduled bed, at the far end of the unit, it would have been the end for me. Barbara Gerbier, a physician's assistant and first member of the SICU staff to arrive at my bedside, thought I was already gone. So did the rest of the team.

A crash cart was rushed to my bed, and my hospital gown and blankets were stripped away. Gerbier, in her first week in the SICU, struggled at first but soon got a line into the artery near my groin so I could be pumped full of fluids to create enough pressure to allow my blood to circulate. I needed five liters of saline fluid. Someone else applied defibrillator paddles, yelled "Clear!" and pressed the Start button, shocking my heart into a sustainable rhythm. I was back. I'd been in cardiac arrest for about two minutes, with no oxygen to the brain. The risk of brain damage starts at three to four minutes.

But then another complication arose. My dilating blood vessels lowered my blood pressure again and brought on ischemia, a restriction in blood supply, which, in turn, caused a shortage of oxygen to vital organs, including my brain—enough of a shortage to damage tissue. To understand ischemia, imagine water flowing through a garden hose. If you partially restrict the end of the hose with your thumb, the pressure in the hose rises and the water shoots out much farther. If you then remove your thumb the flow slows to a trickle. The flow of blood carrying oxygen to my brain—stopped dead during the cardiac arrest—was now only a trickle. I was in ischemia from 9:05 P.M. to 9:22 P.M. Seventeen long minutes.

A ventilator was wheeled over to my bed, and I was intubated, the machine moving breathable air into and out of the lungs. My body desperately needed fluids and medicines. As testament to that, two metal stands were set up next to my bed, bags of medicine attached, and multiple drugs flowed into my body through the lines and tubes in my neck, arm, and groin. These lines were everywhere, and I grabbed at them reflexively, agitated by them, trying to pull them out. A decision was made to put me into a medically induced coma.

The medical team needed time to figure out what was wrong with me, and an induced coma could do just that—buy time. It would also reduce the amount of energy needed by my brain and hopefully save me from brain damage. And it would stop me from pulling out my lines. The nurses quickly attached restraints to my arms and tied them to the side posts of the bed.

This was the scene that Wendy saw when she ran into the SICU. A wild, disorienting, and frightening flurry of activity around a bed just to the left of the entrance. It wasn't Bed 5, but she knew right away it was me in there, surrounded by a dozen nurses and doctors, bright lights, noise, and machines. For a second she froze. Then she started shouting. "What's going on, what's wrong? That's my husband in that bed!" Dr. Arif Chaudhry, the twenty-five-year-old resident on duty that night, turned from the bed and took her by the shoulders, gently but firmly. "You can't be here right now."

Wendy made her way to the waiting room. She couldn't believe what was happening. Just thirty minutes earlier she'd received the most amazing news. Now she was waiting again. As I fought for my life.

Around one A.M. Dr. Karpeh, now out of his scrubs and in street clothes, went to the waiting room. He'd been at my bedside the entire time. He explained that I had not had a heart attack and that they had ruled out internal bleeding. The consensus was that the most likely culprit was allergic anaphylactic shock, the "wild card of surgery." There was probably an antigen in the blood transfused into me, a microscopic substance that had caused an allergic reaction and sent my body into shock and circulatory collapse. Dr. Karpeh said he'd only seen something like this happen once before, six years earlier. He didn't tell Wendy that the patient in that case hadn't survived.

It was all too much—that first awful phone call about the results of the CT scan, two and a half weeks of constant fear, a miraculous five-minute reprieve she hadn't dared hope for, only to suddenly crash headlong into *this*. Wendy couldn't stop crying. Too scared to leave the vicinity of the SICU, she stayed in the waiting room, pulled some seat cushions off nearby chairs, and laid them on the floor. She prayed I'd make it through the night.

In Egypt, the connection between music, religion and healing was so great that their priests were required to become both musicians and physicians.

—Jacqueline Schmidt Peters,
Music Therapy: An Introduction

≡ 3 ≡

The Passion of Wendy
and Bach

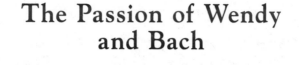

Dr. Karpeh arrived at my bedside a little before seven a.m. on Friday morning. He took one look at me, then at the vital signs computer monitor over my bed, and shook his head. Not good. He scanned my chart and shook his head again. At three a.m. I'd flatlined a second time.

Still in a coma, I'd been put on three pressers, powerful medications to raise my blood pressure. Not just one as it would be if my diagnosis were clear; they were treating and diagnosing me at the same time and couldn't take a chance on not using the right medication. In the early hours of the morning, someone had tried to adjust one of the pressers and the result was nearly catastrophic. I was a house of cards.

A little later, Dr. Karpeh greeted Wendy just outside the SICU entrance. She looked exhausted, her eyes red and swollen from all the crying. "Are you sure you're up for this?" he asked, his voice gentle.

"Yes, I need to see him."

"Then prepare yourself. Andrew does not look like himself right now."

She nodded.

"Remember, most people in a coma can hear. Try not to cry or get agitated when you're with him. If you can't control yourself, you should leave the room until you calm down, okay?"

"Okay." She took a deep breath and exhaled slowly.

They entered the unit, walked the few feet of the foyer, and turned left to face Bed 11. Dr. Karpeh slowly drew open the curtains. It was a different scene from the night before—but no less terrifying. Wendy gasped. She barely recognized me. My entire body was swollen from the fluids pumped into me to get my blood pressure up. I looked like the Goodyear Blimp—bloated and gray, more than she could ever have imagined.

Wendy stared. She took in the IV lines snaking from my arms, neck, and groin, a Foley catheter draining urine into a bag at the foot of the bed, and a tube that ran from my mouth to a ventilator. There was a steady hum coming from the ventilator and constant beeping sounds surrounding the bed. Restraints kept my arms tied to the side posts of the bed. I looked so sick. She gazed at my face, trying to find me, but my eyes were closed, puffy in ashen skin.

Dr. Karpeh pulled a chair up close and spoke softly. "Andrew, you don't have cancer—the mass was benign. You need to rest, stay calm, and be strong. Wendy and I are right here, there are great doctors and nurses in the SICU, and we're all doing our best to take care of you."

Wendy sat down next to me, holding in tears, and stroked my forehead; it was clammy with sweat. Her mind reeled, trying to make sense of what had happened, taking in the number of drugs and machines keeping me alive, the figures flashing on different monitors, the vital signs computer over my bed. What did the numbers mean—what was low, what was high? She fought to stay calm, taking long steady breaths, then looked up at Dr. Karpeh, unable to keep from asking that same question again.

"Is he going to survive?"

"Andrew is very, very sick. We're doing everything we can to keep him alive so his body can recover from the shock. Try and talk to him as much as possible. The sound of a loved one's voice can make a huge difference."

Wendy was flustered. I looked so unlike myself, so far removed from her. What could she possibly say? And how could I hear? She wanted to tell me something that would make me happy, that would motivate me. Then it came. She thought of something so dear to both of us—our dogs. She moved closer to my ear.

"Andrew, I've just thought of the perfect name if we get a third dog. Calvin!"

She knew it was a name I'd love. I'd been addicted to reading the daily comics since I was a boy and my favorite comic strip had been *Calvin and Hobbes*.

Dr. Karpeh smiled and patted Wendy's shoulder.

"I have to go see other patients now, but I'll be checking in throughout the day."

The rest of that Friday, one complication followed another—heart problems, respiratory problems, and constant blood pressure instability. My vital signs were all over the place, my heart rate jumping up and down every other second, never stable. Specialists were called to my bedside. As soon as one issue was resolved, it seemed that another would arise. Wendy was asked to return to the waiting room time and again as doctors fought to stabilize me. At one point, a cardiac specialist was brought in when I went into atrial fibrillation—my heartbeat was chaotic and irregular again. He was able to bring it under control, and on his way out he noticed Wendy sitting, crestfallen, in the hallway outside the SICU. He only had a moment, but, knowing she was my wife, he stopped and said, "This is a marathon, not a sprint." It gave her hope. He went on to his next patient and she returned to Bed 11.

Passing through the curtain she saw Dr. Marvin McMillen, the SICU director, sitting next to me. She'd noticed him the night before, looking like a general commanding troops in a battle.

Now he looked thoughtful. Another life-threatening situation had just developed. The right ventricle of my heart was swelling, decreasing the function of the left ventricle. Dr. McMillen turned to a nurse, frowned, and said, "It's terribly predictable." He sat down, put his head in his hands, and said in a low voice, "Nothing is working. I'm out of ideas."

But he wasn't. He had over thirty years of experience and remembered an old critical care medicine adage: "Better is the enemy of good." Maybe he didn't need to normalize me immediately. Turning to the nurse and resident standing nearby, he said, "For the next thirty minutes, don't do anything."

It worked. The thirty minutes of doing nothing allowed my body to do what was needed on its own. That problem corrected itself.

But I wasn't getting better. In fact, my condition was gradually getting worse. For the rest of that day, almost on the hour, everything that could go wrong did. Cardio, pulmonary, vascular. My vital signs were up and down. Especially concerning was the buildup of lactic acid in my veins, which often results from inadequate blood flow and oxygen delivery to critical tissues and organs.

At six P.M. McMillen headed back to his office and evaluated my case with his chief physician's assistant, Nathan Boucher. He'd rarely seen one this bad.

"I don't think his body can clear the acid buildup. The numbers are off the scale. Usually by now we have a clear trend that the patient is showing signs of recovery. But in this case, we're still struggling to get the slightest improvement. I think this guy is toast."

Sunday, Noon

My third full day in the SICU. I was in Bed 7 now, moved closer to the Nurses' Station so they could keep a close eye on me. No one expected me to survive—Wendy could see it on the faces of the staff. There was no improvement in my condition, no further changes in my treatment. I was still in a coma, bloated and gray. She stared at the vital signs computer screen over my hospital bed. By now she understood what the numbers meant, knew that their volatility showed how precarious my condition continued to be. She watched them flash up and down, hold still for a second, and then move again. They hadn't been stable from the moment I'd arrived. Once again she willed my blood pressure to stabilize. Dr. McMillen had said that would be the first sign of healing. It was hard to keep on hoping.

She looked at the multiple metal stands around my bed, still laden with bags of medicine. Next to them were the IV infusion pumps pushing the fluids through plastic tubes and into my body, all of them painted blue, green, and beige and lit up by glowing red LED lights. Nurse Pilar Baker had made a comment to the other nurses about this "Christmas tree" at my bedside. What Wendy didn't know was that a "Christmas tree" was the sign of a last-ditch effort, that death was likely imminent. Nor did she hear the nurses whisper that the attending physician should be alerted soon to console the "widow." In private, Dr. McMillen called it "the black bunting speech." But she saw and felt the darkening mood around her.

As she looked about, she sank further into despondency. It had been an exhausting three days filled with increasing hopelessness. So tired and frightened; she was running on empty. She didn't know what to do anymore, how to get through to me, or help me. She was all talked out. But as her spirit spiraled downward, she began to feel angry—not at any *person*, just angry at the whole thing. She thought, "Enough is enough already." It revived her fighting instinct.

"All these drugs aren't doing anything. They're keeping you

alive, barely, but they're not making you any better." Her mind raced, trying to imagine what I must be feeling—surrounded by beeping machines, imprisoned in a coma, and dying.

In that moment, she understood that something in the core of my being was broken, but she had no idea how to fix it.

One of the things that had comforted her most these past few days had been talking on the telephone, almost every hour, with my mother. Maybe Sylvia would have an idea of something she could do. Wendy reached for her bag to get her cell phone. Next to it was my iPod. In that split second, out of desperation came inspiration.

Music. Maybe music could save me.

If anything could give me the will to live in this bleak place, it was music. As she lifted the iPod out, she caught sight of Dr. Simon Eiref, the attending physician on duty that morning. He'd just left the OR and was still in his purple surgical scrubs and cap.

"Dr. Eiref," she said. "I think Andrew has lost his will to live. If there's one thing I know about my husband, it's that he loves music more than anything else. It's his passion. We've all been doing everything we can. At this point, I think music is the only thing that could get through to him. I have his iPod here. Please, please—can I play some music for him?"

Dr. Eiref, the associate director of the SICU, a man of few words but with a quick and sharp intelligence, immediately understood. He also knew that everything done in a critical care situation carries a risk.

"Okay, no more than thirty minutes, though. Not too loud. If he shows any signs of agitation, lower the volume, and if that doesn't help, stop the music completely. Put one earbud in for him and put the other in your ear so you can monitor the volume level."

He continued on his way.

Wendy closed her eyes and paused for a moment to say a silent prayer, and then returned to me. As she unraveled the long black earbud cords, she suddenly realized she'd never used an iPod before and had no idea how it worked.

Luckily, Chris, a young medical student, had just stopped by. We'd bonded in the OR before my surgery and he'd come to visit. When he saw Wendy struggling with the iPod he offered to help. He inserted one earbud in my left ear, and the other in Wendy's right.

"Any track in particular you want him to hear?" he asked.

"I have no idea, maybe just try the first thing on the list."

The music was in alphabetical and numerical order starting with "BWV 244 St. Matthew. Johann Sebastian Bach's St. Matthew Passion." The music I'd been listening to on the rowing machine. My favorite piece in the world.

Wendy clicked on the first track and Bach's music began spinning into our ears. Ninety seconds after the flutes and oboes began playing that mesmerizing melody, slowly lifting ever upward, the voices entered, floating heavenward.

Come, ye daughters, help me lament, Behold! Whom? The Bridegroom. Behold him! How? Like a lamb. Behold! What? Behold his patience. Behold!

As the chorus sang, my bride was sitting with her face inches away from her bridegroom, sharing the music that was bonding us together in the darkest moment of our lives.

Bach's masterpiece, some of the most glorious music ever written, tells a story centered on the most basic of human emotions: love, hate, betrayal, and redemption. Wendy barely heard any of it. She sat very still, her eyes focused on my face, watching closely for any sign of agitation. She was on an emotional seesaw. What if it didn't help? What if it made things worse, made me lose all hope? Her body was tense, her jaw clenched as she held her breath, hoping that everything would be okay.

The music reached me.

I'd walked down this street many times. It was peaceful, lined with small tidy homes and well-kept yards. I played for the widow at Christmastime every year. An icy wind blew. I felt very cold inside and pulled my coat tighter. My guitar, in its beat-up case, was so much heavier than usual. I didn't understand why I was walking so slowly, why I felt so tired.

I couldn't remember which house was hers and called out to a man across the street, "I'm here to play for the widow."

Silently, he pointed to the house directly behind me. Yes, of course, the white stucco house, ivy crawling up around the windows and the red brick walkway leading to the front door. I rang the bell. Seconds passed. The door opened slowly. The widow, her red hair now turning gray, her sad blue eyes downcast, moved to the side so I could enter. She walked ahead, leading me through an archway into the dining room.

There it was again, the ancient oak table against the left wall, filled with platters of cookies, cakes, all the sweets of the season. The heavy draperies, thick carpeting, everything was as I remembered it from the past.

She continued ahead to the chair against the far wall and sat, facing me. I took out my guitar. I was so tired and the guitar was so heavy. I couldn't understand why. I sat down, wanting to play, but couldn't. I just sat there, holding the guitar.

Then I heard the music. Beautiful, powerful, soaring music. All of a sudden my hands were moving. I was playing but I had no idea how I could possibly be doing so—I'd never played this music before. What a marvelous thing! I didn't feel tired anymore. I felt so alive, so happy.

I glanced up.

The widow was looking at me. She was smiling.

At the thirty-minute mark, as Dr. Eiref had instructed her to do, Wendy pulled the earbuds out of our ears. There had been no agitation.

She glanced at the computer monitor, then stared. Something had changed. The numbers were not so skittish as before. They were settling down, starting to stay within normal range. Especially my blood pressure, the key to everything else that needed to happen for me to survive. Finally, it was beginning to stabilize. Nurses started to gather around my bed, nurses who'd been so sure just thirty minutes earlier that I was close to death, who'd seen this scenario play out time and time again over the years. They couldn't believe what they were seeing.

Wendy was exhausted but, sensing that something very important had changed, kept glancing at my face, the computer monitor, the nurses. For the first time in days, she smiled. She cried, but they were the tears of hope, if not yet joy. Later the nurses would call it a miracle. The St. Matthew Miracle.

Within another few hours, my vital signs stabilized. By early evening, Dr. Eiref told Wendy, with cautious optimism, that I was "out of the woods." The medical charts, my SICU progress notes report that would wind up being over three hundred pages long, bore witness in precise numbers that the music was the turning point. Before that it was clear that everyone expected me to die. And afterward, everything started getting better. There were no more crises. I never regressed. Three days passed and it was time to bring me out of the coma.

There was an ultimate reality I'd faced three weeks before. The simple reality now was that the passion of Wendy and Bach had saved my life.

India valued music for its mantra-mystic qualities. They discovered that certain sequences of notes produced meditative states, and they experimented and subtly refined these to achieve Samadhi, a superconscious trance. The Hindus believed that this music-induced, mystical, metaphysical state of consciousness helped them achieve oneness with the universe and promoted healthiness of body, mind, and spirit and a purer state of inner awareness.

Already, before the 2nd Century, B.C., the Samaveda told of links between man, music and the cosmos.

—Jacqueline Schmidt Peters,
Music Therapy: An Introduction

☰ 4 ☰

Awakenings

Thursday, 3:00 A.M.

THE WHITE DISK, about three feet across and a few feet in front of me, was blank at first. Then it started spinning clockwise, and landmasses surrounded by oceans came into view. The first signs of life, one-celled organisms appeared. Ancient creatures came and went, each morphing into the next stage. Finally, we arrived—humans. Civilizations, one supplanting the next. Then, just as the Romans appeared, everything went blank. The disk stopped spinning.

Slowly, it came into clear focus. Not a magical disk and not exactly in front of me. It was a light fixture in the ceiling directly over my bed.

I was back in the real world, the inner world of my coma left behind now.

Comprehension followed swiftly. "Those were all *dreams!*" The strange and wonderful things I'd seen, different places, different countries, all those people, those funny, scary, bizarre things. They were all just dreams.

Where was I?

I struggled to think. Dr. Karpeh had said that after the operation I'd be in the Surgical Intensive Care Unit for a day or two. This must be it.

I squinted through the dim light at a clock on the wall. Three o'clock. I didn't hear voices, just constant beeping sounds. It must be early morning. Over my shoulder, I saw a computer monitor suspended from the ceiling, large numbers glowing on the screen. My bed was surrounded by machines and medical devices, chirping and humming. I took it all in.

"This . . . is . . . fascinating!"

I'd learn later that when most people awaken from a coma or from anesthesia in a SICU they are usually disoriented, frightened, even traumatized. Often they feel alienated to such an extent that they have little or no memory of that moment. It's not uncommon to have patients who don't recall anything from their entire stay there.

My fascination soon shifted. I remembered why I was there: I'd just had surgery for pancreatic cancer. A heavy weight pressed down on me, and everything darkened as if someone had dimmed the lights.

From what I'd read online in the last few weeks and the stories I'd heard over the years, I knew I was probably going to die. The question was, how soon? I didn't want to die in this hospital bed. My desire to survive had a very narrow definition: live long enough to die at home. That would require getting out of here as fast as possible, and three things came to mind immediately:

First, make my doctors and nurses laugh as much as possible so when I clicked the little clicker summoning help they'd come quickly. Everyone likes a good laugh.

Second, be a championship-level patient. Do whatever they told me to do *exactly* the way they wanted it.

Third, be 100 percent reality based 100 percent of the time. I wouldn't allow myself to say, "Why me, why did this happen to me?" What a waste of time and energy. I would only focus on getting home.

I drifted back to sleep.

Someone was gently shaking me awake. A powerfully built man wearing dark-blue scrubs said, "I'm here to take an X-ray." He turned and pointed to a big machine on wheels behind him.

As he lifted up my torso to slide a large X-ray plate under me, I said, "Are you Dr. Röntgen?" I'd remembered that it was Wilhelm Röntgen who'd discovered X-rays in the nineteenth century. The technician looked puzzled for a few seconds, then smiled with recognition, and finally burst into quiet laughter.

My get-home-quick plan was off to a good start.

Thursday, 8:00 A.M.

Wendy drew back the curtain. Awake, I smiled and said, "Hi Wendy!" If I could have taken one photograph during that time, it would have been of that moment. She was beyond radiant. She was luminous. She, and everyone else, had spent a week wondering if I would have brain damage if I survived. Not only had I recognized her, I'd spoken her name clearly, without slurred speech.

She pulled a chair up very close. Taking my hand and holding it gently, she said, "I love you." I could see she had something else to tell me—for a few moments she seemed to be looking for the right words. "Your surgery wasn't yesterday—it was eight days ago. You don't have cancer. You went into shock and they saved your life. You were in a coma for a week and they woke you up yesterday. You're going to be okay." She paused, took a deep breath, and then said again, very slowly, "You don't have cancer."

Time stopped for me. A cascade of emotions, thoughts, and memories swirled through my mind. I felt no sense of surprise. For good reason: I wasn't hearing all this for the first time. You hear everything in a coma. It's not processed in the same way as when you're awake and conscious, but somewhere inside I already knew everything she'd just said.

Odd as it may seem, I felt disappointed. Just hours earlier, I'd been a warrior, making a heroic plan to survive long enough to die at home in my own bed. Now I was just another guy who'd been in surgery and would go home and recuperate. This feeling passed very quickly.

Seconds later I was hit with enormous power by the understanding of the word *awesome* in its original meaning: an overwhelming feeling of reverence. I had come as close to death as you can, and I'd received the greatest gift anyone can have bestowed upon them—a second chance at life. I breathed in. But within seconds my emotions were reeling again. I felt a sense of panic. I suddenly thought of my father.

Not of his death in an ICU twenty-five years earlier. But of the survivor's guilt I believe he'd suffered all his life, having made it through the Second World War by a stroke of luck while his friends were shipped out to the beaches of Normandy. He never found a way to pay that forward, to resolve his feelings. He was a happy man in many ways, the kind of person who lit up a room, but I always believed that pressure built up inside of him until his aorta burst and he died twelve days later.

I looked across the way and saw an elderly woman in Bed 12, her face contorted with pain. I heard patients groaning in beds nearby, and the incessant beeping of medical machines. I watched people in street clothes pass my bed, faces grim, most likely on their way to see a loved one who was suffering.

I turned to Wendy and said, "With what happened to me, you can't thank God enough, or your doctors and nurses, or your loved ones. To give thanks you have to *give* something." I looked again at the woman in Bed 12. "This place is gloomy. It needs music. I'm going to come back here with my guitar."

I was thinking only of myself in this moment as the thought of survivor's guilt filled me with trepidation. By returning to the hospital I would attempt to hold it at bay. In war there has always been something called collateral damage: the innocent are killed just because they are in the wrong place at the wrong time. By playing music for the critically ill, I would be committing an act of collateral kindness.

In midafternoon, I started laughing. I was lying there looking up at that light fixture, the formerly mystical disk revealing the secrets of the universe, and listening to the noise of the SICU. Wendy glanced at me, puzzled.

"Now I know who the jazz trio was!"

Even more puzzled, but now laughing, Wendy sat back in her chair. "Okay, Andrew. The jazz trio. What jazz trio?"

I'd already told her, and anyone else nearby, that coma dreams were to regular dreams what a Fellini movie was to a dog food commercial. I now understood one of the recurring coma dreams I'd had. In it, I kept finding myself looking through the window of a darkened jazz club in the basement of a building on Eighth Avenue and Fifty-fifth Street in Midtown Manhattan. The club was always empty except for a trio—a pianist, a bass player, and a drummer, all very cool-looking guys. As I listened to them, I always thought they were playing minimalist music—I actually had that word in mind each time—and I would listen to them for a while until the fade into the next dream.

Laughing louder I said, "The jazz trio was the ventilator machine!"

Wendy thought I was delirious from the drugs still in my system. But I wasn't; I was beginning to discover what goes on when you are in a coma.

Back when the first modern electronic ventilator machines were built in the 1970s, they had warning tones to indicate a malfunction, or a problem the patient was having. Those were repeated beeps. The companies received a lot of feedback from people, especially doctors and nurses, about how annoying those beeps were. So, they programmed little melodic fragments as warning sounds instead.

One of those short melodies I'd heard so many times during

my coma consisted of the following ascending tones: F#-B-E#-F#, with the last note repeated twice. A very angular little tune, especially because of the tritone B to E# (once called a *diabolus in musica*—the devil in music—because of its highly dissonant sound). No doubt programmed by the ventilator manufacturer for the very reason that its angularity would stand out and be more easily heard by the staff. If you don't play an instrument, ask someone to play it for you, and you'll hear why I thought it was jazz. Its short duration and repetition also made me think of minimalism—like the modern compositions of Philip Glass and Steve Reich. There was also a second ventilator melody—a B descending to a G#. That one is a little bluesy. The first riff, the notes going up, is a high-priority signal requiring immediate attention to the patient, whereas the second one is low priority. I was probably hearing it not only from my ventilator; all the machines in the SICU make a veritable orchestra.

If you are in a coma you are most likely on a ventilator machine, and as long as your auditory nerve and auditory cortex are functioning, you are probably hearing those little tunes fairly often. For me, the sounds translated into a "dream" about standing outside a jazz club. But how would they translate to other patients, especially people who weren't musicians? Those repeating tones could be very disorienting, causing strange dreams that were not as captivating as my jazz trio. As I lay there and listened, I realized all the machines made noises of some kind. I thought how nice it would be to, if not replace them, at least mask their discordance with something else. Just hours earlier, I had made the decision to return to the SICU with my guitar and already, though I didn't realize it, I was beginning to think like a medical musician.

I asked Wendy to take out pencil and paper so she could write down the notes of the two tunes made by the ventilator machine. Now that they weren't being played by the jazz trio from my coma dreams they were grating on my nerves. I needed to change them back into pleasing musical pieces. The first riff was so quirky I decided I would write a guitar piece based on that theme. (Still on my to-do list.) The second was easier to handle: I just pretended it was Eric Clapton playing Willie Dixon's old blues number "Spoonful" and sang along with it. Worked like a charm, and I found myself relaxing again.

I was making a very fast recovery. By the end of the afternoon, I walked to the end of the Nurses' Station and back with the help of an aluminum walker, Wendy, and nurse Will Burga. It was my first time out of bed in eight days.

Several doctors and nurses were at work at computers behind the counter. One of them, Dr. Arif Chaudhry, looked at me with a puzzled expression. Then I saw something I would see several times in the next few days. There really is such a thing as seeing someone who thinks they're seeing a ghost. Chaudhry had been on duty that first night when I was rushed into Bed 11, then two days later was rotated out. He'd assumed, as everyone else did, that I was going to die. Seeing me now caused a sudden shock to his nervous system. His eyes popped open wide, his jaw dropped, and his face blanched. But Chaudhry, a very smart young man, quickly recovered his composure. With a mischievous grin, he said, "Eight days ago my shoelaces were higher than your blood pressure."

I began to understand how desperately sick I'd been. Nurses would whisper things like, "We're so happy to see you like this. No one thought you would pull through." I learned there had been two meetings about me in the hospital. Not to understand why I'd gone into shock, but to try to figure out how I'd survived.

Within three days of coming out of the coma, I was assigned a regular room. Dr. Karpeh's chief resident, Dr. Mandy, stopped by to tell me that they were skipping Step-Down, the intermediary unit after the SICU, to send me straight to a regular room. Just a week earlier he had sped me to the SICU as I fought for my life. It was all a bit surreal.

Saturday, 5:00 P.M.

A transporter had been called to take me on another gurney ride, this time out of the SICU and into a regular room on the tenth floor. We said goodbye to all our new friends. A bittersweet moment. These were the people who had saved my life and given Wendy and me extraordinary care. But there was more to it than that. My determination to return to the SICU to play guitar had been reinforced by seeing the camaraderie of the staff, especially the nurses. Having worked as a musician at a lot of different places, I knew how enjoyable it was to work with an A-team. Dr. McMillen had assembled and trained a great staff. I wanted to be around them again.

As we waited, we chatted with respiratory therapist, Jeffrey Vogel, a choral singer in his free time. He told us the hospital had its own music therapy department, one that was world renowned in the field of Music & Medicine. Wendy and I turned to each other and simultaneously said, "How cool is that!"

Louis Armstrong, the famous jazz trumpeter, singer, and entertainer, one of the greatest American musicians of all time, was hospitalized at Beth Israel several times in the last three years of his life and was very grateful for the quality of his care. He loved the place. He'd always been generous in helping others, especially in the area of music, and he continued that generosity with his foundation. In 1994, a grant from the foundation enabled Dr. Joanne Loewy, a music therapist who herself had been hospitalized at Beth Israel for several months, to found the first medical music psychotherapy program of its kind: the Louis and Lucille Armstrong Music Therapy Program. Dr. Loewy still oversees the program while John Mondanaro is clinical director. We were certainly in the right place for what I wanted to do next.

Finally, the transporter arrived. Taking one last look around, I got onto the gurney under my own steam. As we approached the double doors, one of the nurses came over.

"We're so glad you're doing so well, and we never want to see you again!" It wouldn't be the last time I heard this.

Saturday, 10:30 P.M.

A young resident had made a mistake in listening to me before a minor procedure, taking out the surgical drains that removed various fluids from my abdominal wound. She didn't use a painkiller because I said I didn't need one. Within ten minutes I was regretting my decision. A veteran nurse, Karen Gottlieb, came to the rescue and put me on a morphine drip that lasted several hours, catapulting me into hallucinations of a fantastic symphonic version of Procol Harum's "A Whiter Shade of Pale" and a performance of "Sister Morphine" by the Rolling Stones in an outdoor café in Amsterdam.

When the drug wore off in the early hours of the morning, I fell into a deep depression. It was the only time during my stay that I felt the cold fear of death. I was slipping into dysphoria, the opposite of euphoria, a dangerous emotional state for a critically ill patient. You are falling down a well and, worse, you don't care if you come out of it again. Luckily, one floor down, nurse Karen had an intuitive feeling that I was in trouble and came to my bedside. In just five minutes, her soothing voice and her choice of words pulled me back from the brink. Her lesson in how to calm and heal a patient would be invaluable to me as a medical musician.

Sunday, Noon

Dr. Mandy returned again midmorning and regarded me with a warm smile. My progress had been so rapid that there was nothing more they could do for me here. They were sending me home the next day. It was the best news we could have received.

At lunchtime, my roommate received half a dozen guests. He had the bed by the window and mine was near the door. There was just a curtain separating us, and from things I'd overheard I knew he was not likely to survive. Although I could see the strain on his visitors' faces as they passed my bed, I also saw they were determined to make the best of the visit. They'd brought food and beverages and, within a few minutes, there was loud conversation and a lot of laughter. They'd also brought a portable CD player that soon unleashed some really booming, and to me at least, dreadful music.

I couldn't bear to listen to it, but I didn't feel strong enough to take a stroll down the hall. I happened to look at the small table next to my bed and saw that Wendy, who had gone out to get something to eat, had placed my iPod there. Perfect. I'd play something I liked and drown out the other music. I put in the earbuds, and looked at the playlist, and there, first on the list, was my favorite piece. Johann Sebastian Bach's *St. Matthew Passion*, with its double orchestra, a double choir, a slew of soloists, and a huge sound. Just what I needed!

I clicked on the track.

Within seconds, I was overcome with weeping. Not crying—weeping. Music had moved me to tears before from beauty or emotional resonance, but nothing had ever gotten to me as deeply as this. A deluge of tears flowed, and wouldn't stop. As if it was coming from the very core of my being.

I had only cried like this once before in my life—the night my father died. I kept listening and the intense weeping continued. It was completely overwhelming. But I couldn't stop listening. I didn't want to.

After about thirty minutes, Wendy walked into the room. She rushed to me, bewildered. I took out the earbuds.

"I started listening to the *St. Matthew Passion* and just started this weeping, like I'm grieving. I've *never* felt something like this before."

Wendy knew she had to explain. She'd planned to tell me at home, but it was too late for that now. She told me the story of what happened on the third day of the coma. The St. Matthew Miracle, as the nurses were calling it.

I'm glad I found out the story from the music itself. It meant so much more that way. Just as there had been no surprise when Wendy told me what happened the morning I awoke from the coma—because I'd already heard it all—I realized that the body remembers, too.

Later I'd learn that there's a field in cognitive science called "embodied cognition," one that turns on its head the traditional view that thought is an activity that takes place only in the brain. Cognitive scientists posit—and have proved—that thought takes place in the brain, in the body, and in the environment around us. When I listened to the *St. Matthew Passion* again, I believe my body remembered how very close I'd come to death, and it set off my uncontrollable weeping. Weeping that reminded me of my father's death. Suddenly my near death and my father's death had become inextricably linked.

In April 1944, my father had just finished basic training with an infantry company at Fort Dix in New Jersey. One afternoon, the men were playing baseball when my father caught a fly ball and jammed his thumb. He was in so much pain that two of his buddies took him to the infirmary. They left him there. He never saw them again.

A doctor examined him. It was painful but nothing was broken. As he got up to return to his unit the doctor told him he couldn't leave—he'd arrived in the infirmary after five P.M. and the rules dictated he had to stay the night for observation.

At dawn, an officer told my father that his company had received its marching orders at midnight and were already on their way to Europe. He was to remain in the infirmary until he received orders to join another unit.

Five minutes later, a lieutenant walked in and stood in the center of the room to make an announcement. He was the director of the U.S. Army Band stationed at Fort Dix. They were leaving on a tour to play USO shows throughout the South the next day. The band's baritone saxophone player had been badly injured in a car accident the day before and they needed a replacement right away. In a booming voice, the officer said, "Does anyone here play baritone sax?"

My father's hand shot up. He'd played swing fiddle every summer for years with a band in the Catskills and his best friend was the baritone sax player, so he knew the rudiments, and the baritone sax was mainly used for playing harmony, at which he was particularly gifted.

My father got the gig. Within a short time the band voted to make him a permanent member.

I only heard him tell the story twice, once when I was a teenager and again when I was home from college, a fly on the wall in our back room with him and his cronies telling their war stories after a Thanksgiving meal. The other guys were all combat veterans. My dad didn't smile when he told his story. I think he was very uncomfortable. He'd known his unit was heading to D-Day and may well have landed on Omaha Beach. I believe he carried that survivor's guilt until the day his aorta burst.

When Wendy told me what happened the morning I awoke

from the coma, I thought immediately of my father. Now I understood why. Music had saved us both.

A huge thunderstorm had raged beyond the window on the other side of my room, but it was easing off now. Suddenly I heard people shouting, their voices excited, so I hurried as best I could along the hall. Patients and staff gathered in empty rooms, pressed up close against the windows, looking out, and as I approached I saw it, too. The most amazing rainbow, a few hundred feet away, towering over the Empire State Building. I stood and stared, full of hope, that better times lay ahead for Wendy and me.

Monday, 11:00 A.M.

It was noticeably quiet as we entered the SICU. Wendy, me, and the transporter pushing my wheelchair. Halfway down the hallway, six or seven young doctors and nurses faced a man who looked just as Wendy had described. Heavyset, broad-shouldered, about sixty, with sandy gray hair and a close-cropped beard. Dr. Marvin McMillen. Wendy had found out he was back on duty and had gotten us special permission to return to the SICU to see him. He'd been in charge for my first three days there and was central to my survival. Though he knew who I was, I'd never had a chance to see him. We were within fifteen feet when they all turned. No one recognized me, the patient in the wheelchair, and they started turning back—but then Dr. McMillen and a nurse took another look. They recognized Wendy. Now they knew who I was. More double takes followed by that "just seen a ghost" look.

"Dr. McMillen, thank you for saving my life."

McMillen would have none of it. "We just kept you alive long enough so that your body would heal on its own and save your life."

When it was time to go, McMillen smiled and said the standard, "We're very happy you are doing so well and we never want to see you again."

My response was emphatic. "No, I do want you to see me again. I want to come back here with my guitar."

He clearly wasn't expecting that. There was a change in his expression, a distant look on his face. I thought for a moment that he was going to say no. But he didn't.

"Go home, get better, and then call me."

Egyptian priest-physicians referred to music as "medicine for the soul" and often included chant therapies as part of medical practice.

—Jacqueline Schmidt Peters,
Music Therapy: An Introduction

5

Returning

THE SECOND I WAS HOME, I knew exactly where I wanted to go. My guitar was on its stand in a corner of the living room near the front window, and I went straight to it—slowly, leaning on Wendy's arm. It weighed less than four pounds, but when I picked it up it felt more like forty. A Bach Sarabande, a slow movement from the *Second Lute Suite*, was on my music stand, a new arrangement I'd done, intending it to be the first thing I'd work on when we returned home. A perfect, albeit unplanned, choice—the opening melody is nearly identical to the final chorus of the *St. Matthew Passion*.

Within seconds of sounding the first note, I understood what a terrible toll twelve days in the hospital had taken. I felt like a five-year-old who'd just started taking lessons. The slightest movement of my fingers took a huge effort, and even reading the notes on the page was difficult. Within a minute, an intense headache throbbed on the left side of my head. The pain and effort didn't matter, though. I desperately needed to play again.

I plowed on and made it through to the end without stopping. It felt incredibly good to make music, but what would have normally taken me five minutes took fifteen. I put down the guitar, exhausted. But relieved. In the back of my mind I had worried all this time about neurological impairment—that my brain wouldn't be up to the intricacies of reading the score or moving my fingers. But I was lucky. I could still play the guitar! With time and practice, I would be back to my old self and able to get back to work again. I ambled the few yards to the sofa, collapsed onto it, and slept.

The next day I mustered the energy to play the guitar again. Not the Sarabande this time, but a piece by the Brazilian composer Heitor Villa-Lobos. Prelude no. 4. It was Wendy's favorite, and I knew it by heart. In my fifty years of playing guitar, I'd accumulated an extensive repertoire of music that I could play from memory. Not just classical; I loved all kinds of music. Bach, Beatles, Albéniz, Gershwin, and much more. Nearly all my solo performing was done from memory. I knew about three hundred tunes, classical and popular—over twelve hours of music.

I started to move my fingers and felt a sudden stab of pain on the left side of my head as if someone had jabbed me with an ice pick. I got through the first few notes and then stopped. I had to. I couldn't remember more than that. I tried again. Same thing. I tried another piece, a Scarlatti sonata. A note or two, then fade to black. One after another I tried different favorites from all genres, with the same result each time. I had no memory of the pieces. I calmed myself with the idea that maybe it was just the physical and emotional trauma I'd been through, that it would soon correct itself.

Within a few days, I discovered that just six pieces remained in my head, all of them learned before the age of twenty and played often throughout the years. Two Beatles songs, two Bach preludes, and two Spanish pieces. Everything else had completely vanished. I had brain damage after all. I'd have to rememorize everything.

Each day I struggled to get my playing skills back. I needed to return to my steady engagement at the InterContinental Hotel in Midtown Manhattan. It was a union contract with good wages and health and pension benefits. Wendy and I were overwhelmed with the aftermath of serious illnesses: the exhaustion of physical recovery, the logistical nightmares and bills that had piled up while we were focused on life-and-death matters. There were medical follow-ups for both of us, not to mention Wendy's struggle with the awful side effects of Tamoxifen, the breast cancer medication she was taking. The dogs were back by the end of the first week, and although they lifted both our spirits, I couldn't walk them. Nor could I cook, or do any of the many things I took for granted. Wendy was bearing the brunt of it all. I needed to get back to work.

So the one thing I did every day was pick up my guitar and play through the headaches and exhaustion, through the clumsiness of my fingers. I tried every trick in the book to rememorize the music I had lost. Learning two measures at a time, playing pieces and singing along with the bass or melody, starting to memorize from the end part back to the beginning. But nothing worked. Nothing would stick. Before, when I memorized a piece,

I could close my eyes and see the notes on the page. Now, within minutes of struggling to recapture just a few bars of music, I'd close my eyes and see blank paper. Pages of blank paper. It was so strange, like a scene in a bad horror movie, that it actually made me laugh.

I should have gone to see a neurologist, but I felt a combination of hopelessness and fear. What was the point in hearing what I already knew: my brain was damaged. I would just have to play from sheet music. It wouldn't be a problem at the Inter-Continental, but my concert days were over—I only played from memory in concerts.

Fear of eviction is a great motivator. Less than a month after I left the hospital, I was back to my gig. I needed a lot of help. Taxi drivers were unfailingly kind when I explained why I needed the help getting things in and out of the trunk; I had great friends at the hotel—every night someone carried my guitar and amp; and so I managed. No one said anything about me bringing sheet music, and, although I knew my playing was not what it had been, it was good enough.

Later, in speaking with Dr. Mark Jude Tramo, neurologist and an expert on music and the brain, I found out what had most likely happened. The doctors in the SICU didn't take brain scans as they fought to save my life. Both sides of my body were moving, which indicated no catastrophic damage, and they had other issues to deal with—so Tramo could only make a surmise about my brain damage.

His view was that the cardiac arrest followed by seventeen minutes in ischemia had caused enough of a shortage of oxygen to my brain that I'd suffered bilateral hippocampal damage, a fairly common result from hypoxia, or oxygen starvation. The hippocampus, a horseshoe-shaped area of the brain found in both hemispheres, is part of the limbic system, a system associated with memory and emotions. The hippocampus itself is involved in the processes of forming, organizing, and storing memories.

Bilateral damage to the hippocampus, as in my case, is therefore likely to affect memory function, and Tramo believed I'd experienced both anterograde and retrograde amnesia. For me, anterograde amnesia affected my ability to memorize new music (generate new memories) after my recovery, and retrograde amnesia meant I couldn't remember how to play the music I'd memorized before I went into cardiac arrest.

It is interesting that my amnesia affected only my musical memory. I was able to form new memories, both autobiographical and factual, outside of music memorization, and I didn't seem to have any difficulties in recalling memories from my past. I was very lucky. There are studies about patients with terrible cases of anterograde amnesia, the most famous being that of a patient known widely as HM (Henry Molaison). In 1953, a surgeon removed part of twenty-seven-year-old HM's brain, including both his hippocampi, to treat him for severe epilepsy. The treatment worked but left him with severe anterograde amnesia. He was unable to form new memories of any kind for the rest of his life (he died in 2008), and described his condition, "Every day is alone in itself, whatever enjoyment I've had, and whatever sorrow I've had. . . . It's like waking from a dream."

According to Dr. McMillen, "Brain damage caused by lack of

oxygen will often target the part of the brain used most." For someone like me, who'd been memorizing music and playing from memory for the last fifty years, the hippocampus was clearly my Achilles' heel.

Surprisingly—and fortunately—there was no inability to remember how to read music and play the guitar. And there were those six pieces I could still play from memory, all learned before the age of twenty. I was an example of what doctors call "a fascinoma," or in layperson's language, an interesting case.

"You hadn't lost the complex skills needed to play familiar music," said Tramo, "as long as you had written music to guide you via brain connections integrating the work of visual neurons in the occipital lobe with the work of neurons in the frontal and parietal lobes that carry out the motor, kinesthetic, and spatial processes needed to perform the piece. Yet when you tried to access *memories* of familiar music stored in hippocampal neurons in the medial temporal lobes, they were gone, unreadable, and/or inaccessible to motor, kinesthetic, and spatial neurons."

It was as if the file cabinet where I stored the scores of memorized music was now empty. Or the path to that file cabinet was blocked. Empty or blocked? Didn't matter.

As for those six pieces I could still play from memory, Tramo explained, "Ribot's Law, hypothesized in 1881 by Théodule Ribot, states that there is a time gradient in retrograde amnesia. In your case, the closer you learned the piece to the time of your clinical death, the more likely you were to lose it."

When I mentioned that I'd learned all the pieces before I was twenty and I'd always played them on a regular basis, he added, "What you're saying is not 'science,' not 'data.' But, for researchers like me, it's valuable information. Only *you* know the timing of what you learned."

I continued to use the survival philosophy I had created in the SICU. Be 100 percent reality based 100 percent of the time. The reality? I couldn't play from memory anymore or memorize new pieces no matter how hard I tried. But, I could still make music. Eventually I ceased all efforts to relearn from memory and stoically accepted my fate. The silver lining of clinical death was quite useful for coping with this loss: I could play, I could read, I wasn't dead.

As you turn to enter the offices of the Louis Armstrong Center for Music and Medicine, the first thing you see is a poster-sized photograph of a young Louis Armstrong, etched in glass. He's seated, holding his trumpet, elegantly dressed, smiling radiantly. I was early and stood looking at him for a few minutes. I found it tremendously inspiring.

I was meeting with Dr. Joanne Loewy, head of the music therapy program. As I'd promised when leaving the hospital, I had called Dr. McMillen a few weeks earlier and he'd referred me to Loewy. She would have the final say as to whether to allow a former patient, a professional musician with no training as a music therapist, to play in the SICU, the place where many of the sickest patients in a hospital can be found.

The music therapy program, under Loewy's direction, provides a wide range of services in many areas of the hospital, and it also offers outreach programs within the community. Her team—one medical doctor, seven music therapists, twelve graduate interns, two international scholars, and three research fellows—works alongside the doctors and nurses offering a music-based approach to healing that complements medical treatment. If I were to be allowed to return as a musician, I would not be working directly with them. I would only be going into the SICU.

Loewy has conducted research in sedation, assessment, pain, asthma, and neonatal intensive care music therapy. A study published in 2013 details the music therapy work she and her team have undertaken in eleven hospitals with premature babies by replicating the auditory environment of the womb and also in providing music psychotherapy to their fragile parents by instructing them how to use their voices and meaningful lullabies from their family culture.

Loewy, a woman in her forties with curly brown hair and intense eyes, greeted me with a smile and asked me to wait in the adjoining room. I walked into a small studio filled with a collection of musical instruments, some familiar and some I'd never seen before: guitars, a piano, percussion instruments, an Australian Aboriginal instrument called a didgeridoo, and more. I'd brought my guitar and got it out and tuned up. Within a minute or so, I began playing the Prelude from Bach's *First Cello Suite*— one of the pieces I could still play from memory. Halfway through, Loewy walked in, and I gathered from her expression that I'd picked the right piece.

As she sat down, she told me that particular prelude was her all-time favorite piece of music. Score another one for playing Bach in the right place at the right time.

She already knew the essentials of what I'd been through as a patient, and she began talking immediately about what would be the most important things to focus on about playing in a SICU. To listen to everything in the room from the moment you arrive until you leave; to be alert for the unexpected; to be able to respond in an instant to what's needed; and, most important, summed up in two words: you were there to be *soothing* and *healing,* and those two words must always be in the forefront of all your thoughts and actions.

As she explained how different playing in a hospital would be, especially a SICU, from anything I'd ever done before, I realized I was dealing with a whole other kind of intelligence. As a professional musician, I've known many smart, even brilliant, musicians, but Loewy was talking now about music and the brain, data, studies, working with a medical team, and, most important of all, that lives were at stake with the audience I'd be playing for. The degree of focus and attention to detail would have to be at a level beyond anything I'd ever done.

Within a few more minutes I felt she would say yes to my request, but something was weighing on my mind. She saw it, and asked if I had a question.

"I really just have one concern, that because I'm not a music therapist I won't be fully accepted by you and your team."

She smiled, shook her head a little, and said, "You'll learn from us, and we'll learn from you." Her response moved me because of the generosity of spirit it revealed.

She did give her permission, something for which I will always

72 • Waking the Spirit

be grateful. Neither of us knew at that moment where this would all lead, whether it would just be the passing desire of a former patient, or something more than that.

No matter. I was going back to the SICU with my guitar.

The use of music for curing mental disorders reflected the belief that it could directly influence emotion and develop character. Among the notables of Greece who subscribed to the power of music were Aristotle, who valued it as an emotional catharsis, and Plato, who described music as the medicine of the soul.

—Jacqueline Schmidt Peters,
Music Therapy: An Introduction

6

Goin' Home

Six months and a day after Wendy played Bach's *St. Matthew Passion* for me, I walked through Stuyvesant Square, a small gem of a park just across from Beth Israel Medical Center.

The park felt familiar, though I hadn't been there before, with its cast-iron fence, blue stone fountain, and the statue of Bohemian composer Antonín Dvořák in a quiet corner. He'd lived nearby in the 1890s and written his famous New World Symphony there. The spiritual "Goin' Home," one of Wendy's favorite songs, is based on the famous Largo theme from the symphony. Wendy was very much on my mind as I crossed the park. She'd spent a few minutes here each day last summer, taking a break from the intensity of the SICU.

Now I was going back. I breathed in the sharp January air, nervous to be heading to the place where I had almost died, not sure how I'd react. I was equally nervous to be returning to play music. While it was exciting to think about helping and healing people, part of me wondered how I could do that without any training, how I'd fit back in to the world of the SICU. Lost in thought, I entered the hospital building and headed toward the third floor.

Out of nowhere, a young woman's face came to mind, and I remembered the first time I'd heard about music's power to heal. One afternoon in the spring of 1974, I was walking through the music building at Stony Brook University. I was a senior, the first classical guitarist to major in music even though there wasn't a guitar teacher on the faculty yet. I took private lessons off-campus with a well-known teacher, Jerry Willard, and did a lot of independent study work. The young woman, a junior, approached me. Petite, with thick brown curly hair, her dark eyes sparkled with incredible intensity and excitement. She'd just returned from a music therapy conference at New York University, and she was on fire about what she'd learned. We talked for an hour. It was the single most vivid conversation I can recall from my college years. I'd long ago forgotten her name, but I remembered still her boundless enthusiasm about the power of music to heal.

I stepped off the elevator, my guitar case strapped to my back, and turned toward the entrance to the SICU. I paused and looked at the large emerald-green tiles embedded, every few feet, in the floor. The melody of "Over the Rainbow" played in my head, bringing a smile—I felt like I was going back to see the Wizard of Oz.

I pushed open the double doors and was immediately hit by the wave of sound that is so specific to a SICU. And the smell. Clean; almost too clean. I turned left, and there it was. Bed 11.

My bed. I walked past, slowing down, staring, like a driver rubbernecking. The bed was open so I could take my time.

"Andrew . . . you're back!" Nurses Madelene Castro and Rosievic Hamilton had spotted me. They had cared for me the first morning I was fully awake after the coma. I hurried over to them, delighted.

"We never get to see our success stories. No one ever comes back," said Madelene. I could see in their faces how much it meant to have a former patient return and offer *them* something.

Dr. Loewy had suggested I take a few minutes to walk the room before starting to play. To look at the patients and staff, listen to the sounds, and try to take in everything.

The rectangular unit had a walkway shaped like an inverted letter *E* without the middle bar. It ran between the twelve curtained beds, and at its center stood the Nurses' Station. Many of the patients were intubated—some sleeping, some awake. Almost all the beds were full. I recognized the different machines—the ventilators, IV infusion pumps, oxygen tanks, a dialysis machine hooked up to a patient. It all looked as familiar as if I'd been here yesterday. But I knew that for the patients this was far from being a familiar environment. In fact, a SICU can be so anxiety-inducing that many patients are unable to recall a moment of their stay there.

I chose a central spot from where I'd be heard throughout the unit and took out my guitar, my music stand, and my music folder marked BACH. A deep breath, and then I started to play. Months earlier, I'd decided on this first piece, and I'd learned it specifically for this moment. The famous chorale melody that appears five times in the *St. Matthew Passion*. A symbolic choice, for sure, but one that would be recognizable to a lot of people because

Paul Simon borrowed the melody for his beautiful song, "American Tune."

I looked up for a moment halfway through and saw many heads turned my way. It felt great to be here. At long last, this show was on the road.

I started to keep a journal that first day, and it shows I spent an hour in the SICU, playing, besides more Bach, some early-nineteenth-century European guitar music, Brazilian *choro* music of the 1930s (sometimes described as the New Orleans jazz of Brazil), some Gershwin, and some of my own improvisations. I followed my instincts in my musical choices to soothe and heal based on my time as a patient and my many years as a performing musician. People come to a SICU for one basic reason: they are critically ill patients who've had major surgery and need round-the-clock monitoring. Often they share the same feelings of pain, fear, loneliness, and exhaustion.

My first decision was to provide variety. By playing different kinds of music, I thought I would likely please more patients in the room. Variety and positive energy. I kept my playing at a medium tempo in a major key with a flowing steady rhythm. At the very least, it drew the patients' attention away from the incessant beeps of the medical machines. Later I'd learn that playing like this was a good choice. It matches the human heart, when beating in its normal range.

As I got down to the last minutes of the session, I glanced up to see Madelene and Rosievic observing the nearest patients. They looked from the patients, to the computer screens showing the vital signs, and then back to the patients. I knew the monitors displayed heart rate, blood pressure, oxygenation rate, and respiration rate. I remembered the nurses' constant monitoring of them during my SICU stay. Each vital sign has a normal range—the ones that seemed the most important were heart rate (60–100 beats a minute) and blood pressure (120 over 80 or less—low blood pressure begins below 90 over 60).

Rosievic and Madelene turned to each other and exchanged knowing glances. Even to my untrained eye, the patients seemed more relaxed than when I'd started playing. I asked if they thought the music was helping and they nodded. Rosie gave me a pat on the back and headed to another bedside; Madelene smiled and did the same.

I'd just found a new path to express myself as a musician, one that was unlike anything I'd done before. It was about making music solely to help others, and it felt really good.

Anxiety is one of the common denominators in a SICU, and with good reason. Patients there are recovering from serious surgery and may have an unclear prognosis. They are far from home and loved ones, and they have little control over their present—or future—circumstances. The body's biological reaction to such feelings of stress is to power up the fight-or-flight response and release stress hormones into the blood. The body then prepares itself to fight or flee with the help of rapid breathing and a higher heart rate to increase the supply of oxygen and glucose to the brain. Blood vessels are constricted to send more blood to the body's core, temporarily raising blood pressure. Which is all fine if there is a specific threat. But generalized anxiety means that patients in a SICU are often in a constant state of "fight or flight," with high heart rate and high blood pressure—which can negatively impact their recovery.

Numerous research studies document examples of music reducing anxiety in various medical settings and bringing on such physiological changes as lowered heart rate and blood pressure. In the summer of 1977, Dr. Roland Droh, director of the Department of Anesthesiology at a hospital in Lüdenscheid, Germany, asked young medical student Ralph Spintge to study ways of reducing anxiety, stress, and pain before, during, and after surgery. Since then, using operating rooms, anesthesia rooms, and surgical waiting rooms wired for music, Dr. Spintge has studied music's anxiolytic (anxiety-reducing) properties in over 160,000 surgical patients using state-of-the-art research protocols. These robust research standards and guidelines ensure that specific music interventions can be applied and then replicated, enabling scientific evidence to be gathered. Results based on research over the last thirty years show clear physiological changes when patients listen to music before, during, and after surgery, such as a decrease in heart rate and arterial blood pressure, a decrease in respiration flow and oxygen consumption, and reduced nausea and sweating, all indicating lower anxiety levels.

Music reaches neural networks, including some of the most primary and lowest-on-the-evolutionary-calendar-of-development parts of the brain such as the brain stem, the cerebellum, and the amygdala. Music then initiates brain stem responses that, in turn, regulate heart rate, pulse, blood pressure, body temperature, and muscle tension in much the same way as a fight-or-flight response—"stimulating" music heightens sympathetic arousal (heart rate, pulse, and breathing) whereas "relaxing" music decreases it—although there can be exceptions to this.

As a musician, and especially as a musician saved by music, it made sense to me that music could make people feel less anxious. Lullabies have been sung to babies to soothe them to sleep from time immemorial, and many people turn to music to lift their spirits on a daily basis. My goal as a medical musician was to undercut the anxiety by providing a positive distraction, partially masking the noise of the machines, and reminding the patients that they are part of the world beyond the SICU. If I could affect their physiological response along the way, that would be a bonus—a bohemian's rhapsody!

One Friday afternoon, a little over two months after my return, I was setting up when a nurse gave me a message. Dr. McMillen had left it for me before going off duty. I should go to Bed 9 as soon as I arrived; he thought the patient there was slipping into dysphoria.

I still remembered the cold fear of my own brush with this deep depression, and I knew now how dangerous a condition it was in the SICU, especially for older patients. They could slide suddenly into it and never regain their equilibrium. I'd read that music offers a real clinical benefit to patients suffering from depression. I hoped I could help.

I'd seen the patient in Bed 9 earlier in the week. We called him Mr. G. He was a black man in his seventies with longish gray hair and a grizzled beard. He was very cheerful the first time

I saw him, telling everyone in sight that he was a musician and even singing as people walked by. He'd been doing well, and there were some other very critical patients, so I hadn't gone to his bedside. He was decidedly less cheerful the second time I saw him. I knew he was a jazz musician, a saxophonist—I'd recognized his name. He'd been in New York a long time and was a highly respected sideman, a musician in a supporting role who can make the difference in a band sounding great, not just good.

When I went over to Bed 9 now, Mr. G was in a bad way, writhing in the bed, his face contorted. His nurse Penny told me that although his eyes were shut tight he was awake. She thought it was more psychological suffering than physical pain. Earlier, he'd been talking about his fear of dying.

As I looked at him, I tried to figure out how to help. How could I reach this fellow musician and pull him out of that deep sadness and fear? I remembered the way Nurse Karen Gottlieb had spoken to me, the care she had shown. I wanted to do that for this patient. I went and got my folder of old jazz standards, tunes I used to jam on with a dear friend, a sax player, and, instead of pulling up a chair and sitting as I normally did, I stood in front of Mr. G's bed. I started slow with some solo arrangements of lyrical tunes—"Smoke Gets in Your Eyes," "Misty," one or two others. Within a few minutes, the writhing slowed, and then stopped, and the pained expression on his face started to disappear. I had his attention. He was listening to music he'd certainly played many times. Now I wanted him to do more than listen. I wanted him to think about playing.

I switched from a solo style, left out the melody part, and began to play only the chords of the tunes. I wanted him to imagine an ensemble. The guitar, like the piano, can be a self-contained unit, meaning it can play the melody, harmony, and bass line simultaneously. So I figured if I left out the melody and went to chords maybe that would send a signal to Mr. G. I moved to tunes with faster tempos now, as well. "Ain't Misbehavin'," "All the Things You Are." By the time I got to "Take the 'A' Train," Penny and I both saw a remarkable change in his face. His eyes remained closed, but his brow began to furrow, just as a musician's would when he is deeply in the flow of playing. You can't go into someone's mind and see them playing a saxophone solo, like a CT scan can show the details of the cerebral cortex, but it sure looked to me like Mr. G was on a bandstand, playing his horn full tilt. The signal had gotten through. I'm convinced he was playing the melody.

I continued playing music in the same vein for another thirty minutes, the longest session I had done yet for one patient. Penny, looking at the vital signs monitor over the bed, told me there was a noticeable improvement. His heart rate and blood pressure had been very high, and now they were back in the normal range. Some of his anxiety and stress had ebbed away. More important, as an experienced nurse, she could tell that he was moving past a crisis. The music had done more than the sedatives had been able to accomplish. By getting Mr. G to interact, he had reengaged in his life and reconnected to a core part of himself. He was pulling himself up from the bottom of the well.

Music had intervened at just the right moment for Mr. G and had brought about a dramatic change in his health. I was deeply moved. And amazed.

I found out later from McMillen that Mr. G had pulled

through and, although still critically ill, had shown no more signs of dysphoria in the remaining week he was in the SICU. It was astonishing to me that forty-five minutes or so of music could have turned the ship around to that degree. McMillen explained that there is a blossoming effect once things start moving in the right direction. He was an avid sailor in his college years and once explained this effect to me in another way. "Once you catch the wind in your sails, you can get to where you want to go!" He had told me that was what happened when I listened to the *St. Matthew Passion.*

Although I had long since stopped staring at Bed 11 as I walked into the SICU, I hadn't yet lost the feeling that I was there once. And that I could be again one day. I definitely felt a connection with all the patients in the SICU. However, Mr. G was the first person who really made me think back to what had happened when I was pulled out of my coma. I saw how music reached beyond everything that was going on with him, mentally and physically, found his essence, and pulled him back. And it resonated. Because somehow, that had happened to me, too. Music intervened for both of us, stabilized us, and enabled the doctors and nurses to do their job. It was impressive. And inspiring.

Soon after playing for Mr. G, I received an email from Dr. Loewy. She'd come up to the SICU a few times to observe me sight unseen. She and the medical team weren't taking any chances given where I was playing, and the fact that I had no formal training. The email was very encouraging—she thought I had a natural talent for this kind of work. And she had a question: Would I be interested in becoming a music therapist?

The idea instantly struck a positive note. I got quite excited, thinking about new possibilities. Loewy explained that I'd have to go back to school, preferably for a two-year program to get a degree, and recommended several universities with highly regarded programs. I went right to the Web sites of each school. The music courses looked like fun, but then I saw a lot more. A lot of courses. A lot of work. A lot of . . . homework. Many people have nightmares that they are back in high school or college and are totally unprepared for a big exam the next day. I started having one right then and there as I stared at my computer screen. Uh-uh. No. Not gonna happen. One of the primary reasons I became a musician was so I could sleep late every morning.

But, I loved playing in the SICU and wanted to keep doing it. I'd also realized in reading the university Web sites that I was part of a bigger world, one of music, medicine, and healing, and I liked that. So the question now was: If I wasn't going to be a music therapist, what was I going to be? There is an old expression: "Don't be an amateur psychologist." I didn't want to be an amateur music therapist. So, then, what was I?

"Medical musician." That was the first moment I thought of how to describe to others what I was doing. There is no such title in the world of music therapy, or in the bigger field of Music & Medicine, but it fit what I'd already started doing. I'd been using the skills I'd developed as a professional musician and the experiences I'd had as a critically ill patient, and I was finding my way to applying them in the SICU.

It made sense in another way, as well. Music therapists are trained to work in many different environments: in hospitals, rehabilitation centers, hospices, schools, and so on. I was only interested in one thing: working in a critical care unit. It's what I knew, what I identified with, what I was drawn to.

The American Music Therapy Association (AMTA) states that music therapists "assess emotional well-being, physical health, social functioning, communication abilities, and cognitive skills through musical responses; design music sessions for individuals and groups based on client needs using music improvisation, receptive music listening, song writing, lyric discussion, music and imagery, music performance, and learning through music; participate in interdisciplinary treatment planning, ongoing evaluation, and follow up." This was way beyond the scope of what I was doing in the SICU.

In speaking with Al Bumanis, AMTA's director of communications, I charted my journey as a medical musician. He was very encouraging.

"The increasing awareness of the medical community, especially in recent decades, of the therapeutic value of music is a great thing. We need people like you," he said. "In many places, we simply can't keep up with the need for music, let alone music therapy. So when we have artists like you who are under the supervision of an established music therapy department, who understand the role of being a visiting artist, an adjunct that reinforces the existing clinical music therapy program, it can be considered a very good thing for the overall treatment milieu."

It felt good to be appreciated.

Around this same time, I noticed that the degree of concentration needed to play music in the SICU was much greater than anything I'd ever known before as a musician. I was playing in a room where the difference between life and death could be counted in seconds, and I had to be exceptionally careful every moment I was there. At the end of each session, though, I felt invigorated. I'd come home and tell Wendy that my brain felt good. Sort of the way you feel after a vigorous workout in the gym. Those sharp pains I'd felt when I first started playing were long gone.

I was becoming quite addicted to these music sessions in the SICU.

The Romans adopted the Greek philosophy regarding the beneficial moral, ethical, medicinal and healing influences of music. For example they believed that music could cure snakebites, combat pestilence, and aid in curing insomnia.

The physician Aeslepiades treated insanity with harmonious sounds and calmed recalcitrant mobs by a change in music or by playing a certain kind of music.

—Jacqueline Schmidt Peters,
Music Therapy: An Introduction

7

Everything Vibrates

THOUGH I WAS an avid reader, especially of music and military history, my knowledge of the history of music and medicine extended to just three musicians with a connection to healing.

From an early age, I knew the Bible story of David playing the lyre to soothe the foul moods of King Saul when the "evil spirit" overcame him. David is often described as playing the harp because of an erroneous translation of the Hebrew word for the instrument he played, the *kinnor,* which is actually very much akin to the Greek lyre. The lyre and harp have several differences, including their construction; the lyre more closely resembles the guitar in the way it's made and played. A lyrist used a plectrum, the equivalent of a modern guitar pick, and generally more than one string at a time was sounded, like a guitarist strumming chords. However, as a ten-year-old boy, my attention was much more riveted by the scene where, in his jealousy, Saul threw his spear at David, barely missing him. That summed up that story for me for a very long time.

The second musician was someone whose music I knew well, the harpsichordist/composer Domenico Scarlatti. Born in 1685, he was an exact contemporary of J. S. Bach. Guitarists—who, according to one of my college professors, are the "consummate thieves" of the music world because we "steal" so much music originally written for other instruments—love to take Scarlatti's music and arrange it for themselves. I've done it dozens of times. From about the age of thirty-four until his death in 1757, he was the personal musician and teacher for Princess Maria Bárbara of Portugal, who became a superb harpsichordist under his tutelage. She later became the queen of Spain. He played for her almost daily, and apparently, with his music, he helped keep her depression under control.

The third musician was better known as one of the greatest mathematicians and philosophers of all time—Pythagoras, born in Samos, Greece, in the late sixth century BCE. When reading about him, as a music major in college, I noted that he was also a highly accomplished musician. He played the kithara, a member of the lyre family of instruments, and, most interesting to me, an ancient form of the guitar. In modern Greek, the word *kithara* has come to mean "guitar." It was considered a virtuoso's instrument, requiring a great deal of skill. Years later, when I switched from the standard six-string guitar to the eight-string guitar with its added bass strings and deeper resonance, I remembered that Pythagoras had gone against centuries-old tradition and added an eighth string to his seven-stringed kithara to widen the range of his instrument. Greek society held the number seven as sacred, and the addition of the octave disturbed the symbolism of the seven modes of music and the seven planets. However, Pythagoras's standing in a society that revered knowledge and learning protected him from any negative reaction to this adaptation, radical for its time. I felt a kinship with him for that eighth string alone.

He was also a pioneer in the history of musical temperament, which in laypeople's terms involves a series of developments in how to tune musical instruments.

Pythagoras was one of the first to recognize the profound effect of music upon the senses and emotions. He developed his own music healing method, which he called "musical medicine." Music was a core element of the beliefs of his followers, the Pythagoreans. They started each day with music to clear the mind from sleep and prepare for the coming day, and they ended the day with music that was soothing, relaxing, and conducive to rest.

Dr. Bryan Hunter is a past president of the National Association for Music Therapy and the official historian of the American Music Therapy Association. He is also chair of the Creative Arts Therapy Department and director of graduate music therapy at Nazareth College in Rochester, New York. I stumbled upon his name online and arranged to speak with him about the history of music and healing. I had discovered a wealth of information on the subject and wanted to discuss it with an expert. It had made no small impression on me that all the doctors and nurses I knew in the SICU said they learned the most, and best, by talking to each other.

Dr. Hunter started our conversation by confirming that music in medicine is nothing new. "There's a pretty close relationship," he said, "with music and medicine going all the way back to antiquity that stays pretty close until we get into the eighteen hundreds. Then, as physicians developed more advanced understanding of the cellular and biological facts of the human body, music separated from medicine just as a separation developed of treating physical symptoms and treating the mind. That separation stayed in place until the nineteen nineties or so when we get to the notion of 'mind-body medicine.'"

"Are you are referring," I asked, "to what is known as integrative medicine?"

"Yes. There was an epiphany from scientific research, some of it done at the University of Rochester School of Medicine where I was visiting faculty, particularly by David Felten, M.D., Ph.D., and Robert Ader, Ph.D., that physiological nerve connections between the mind/brain going back to the body would actually influence the status of the physical body based on the physiological/emotional status of what was going on in the mind."

This spoke to me directly about music and the brain, and music and healing. As music stimulates different areas of the brain, it can affect physical changes in the body and the mind.

"The close relationship of music and medicine lasted for several millennia at least and then the 'modern science' of the nineteenth century created a chasm . . . and now modern science starting in the late twentieth century strengthens the validity of the connection of music and medicine with neurobiological research," he continued.

This cutting-edge research is starting to convince the medical world of music's place in it. I see it every time a doctor says to me, "Music: the newest thing in medicine."

I wanted to go back to antiquity with Hunter as my guide. I'd reread the Bible story about David and Saul in the original Hebrew, eight years of yeshiva education having not gone completely to waste after all, and noticed some things I'd never thought about before.

"If you go back and look at the first book of Samuel, chapter sixteen in the Old Testament . . . you'll find some very interesting things related directly to contemporary music therapy practice," he said. "What we learn in verse sixteen is that Saul's servants, not his doctors, suggest finding a musician, someone who specifically plays the kinnor, the lyre, not a harp as you point out it is often mistranslated. So, it's clear that music is known to have healing powers not just by the experts, but also by the laypeople. So it may well have been a common practice.

"Also, they ask for a stringed instrument, so there is clearly an association with the healing power of the lyre. Finally, the wording the servants use is someone who 'knows' how to play, indicating not just anyone who 'can' play, and this is then made absolutely clear in the next verse when Saul says, 'Provide me now with a man who plays well.' In other words they wanted to have really good music!"

I laughed. "I love it, that's great, they wanted good music and for good reason. If they'd brought Saul a lousy player he might have thrown a spear at them!"

Hunter had one more thing to add. "Yes, but before the story moves ahead to that, there's another thing that's very interesting. It says that the king became very fond of David and made him his sword bearer."

As he pointed out, the king must have trusted David—you don't give a weapon to somebody you don't trust. In contemporary music therapy, the relationship between the therapist and patient is extremely important, and based on trust.

"So there you have an ancient story with important links to contemporary music therapy practices," added Hunter.

Next I wanted to talk about Pythagoras. It seemed to me that so much about music and medicine could be traced back to him. Hunter confirmed this, stating, "Both the history and science of music and medicine are integrally related and the starting point is Pythagoras. . . . Pythagoras essentially laid the foundation for the entire field of what we today call acoustics. He was the first to discover the manner in which things vibrate and the relationship of those vibrations and the mathematical relationships of the vibrations. Basically, when you look through this history, music was being used as a treatment that was congruent with the contemporary thought about illness, the current theory of the illness."

Hunter explained that the major leap that Pythagoras's teachings and discoveries made are summed up in his understanding that "everything vibrates." His belief that a specifically prescribed use of music could benefit one's health is the basis for all music and medicine, from his time to today. He explored clinical applications of music to treat patients who were mentally ill and introduced treatments in which "musical medicine" was central in promoting health.

He was one of the first musicians to recognize the therapeutic power of music and was convinced that the music of the human organism would respond to sympathetic vibration—a harmonic phenomenon where a formerly passive string or vibratory body responds to external vibrations to which it has a harmonic likeness, such as bridges that have collapsed from armies of soldiers all marching in step at the exact same vibrational frequencies, or how singing at the same vibrational frequency of a crystal glass can shatter it.

A few weeks later, Hunter and I had another phone call. I was interested now in hearing from him about the development of modern music therapy, especially as his professional career was right at the heart of it. I knew already that a big impetus to getting it started as a profession began during World War I and continued in World War II when it was discovered that having musicians, amateur as well as professional, play in hospitals for wounded soldiers and sailors was found to be very helpful in many ways, both physiologically and psychologically.

"The antecedents of modern music therapy began well before the wars," said Hunter. "There was a study on Blackwell's Island in the early eighteen hundreds in New York City, now called Roosevelt Island, when they observed musicians coming in and playing for patients who had mental illness and physicians watching and studying the patient responses. It was the first documented music therapy research in an institutional environment. There were many efforts along these lines throughout the country."

Between my phone calls with Hunter, I'd found out something of great importance. During the Great Depression there was a Federal Music Project, one of the New Deal programs from the Roosevelt era set up to provide employment in the aftermath of the Great Depression and that included employment projects in the arts—music, theater, visual art, and so on.

Hunter elaborated, "One of the interesting things about that project was they didn't want that money to be used to pay musicians to play for Broadway shows, for instance. This was another piece of the foundational history of music therapy—because during the Depression you had musicians being paid by the Federal Music Project to go out and play and one of the places they went to play was in hospitals.

"Music education and music therapy activities . . . were conducted in community centers, settlement houses, orphanages, hospitals, and prisons. It was apparent that strong support for music therapy existed in the New York City metropolitan area during the height of the Depression. That further established the use of medical musicians."

Some hospitals—for instance, Utica State Hospital in upstate New York—began to hire musicians to come in and play and, in about the 1940s, there was the general thought that it would be helpful to provide formal training.

The first academic program was started in 1944 at Michigan State College, now Michigan State University, by psychiatrist Dr. Ira Altshuler, an important figure in music therapy. Earlier, in 1938, Altshuler had initiated one of the first large-scale music therapy programs for people with mental illness in the United States, combining psychoanalytic techniques with music therapy methods. He trained many music therapy interns, including Esther Goetz Gilliland, who went on to become president of the National Association for Music Therapy.

Three national music organizations established committees to look at the idea of formal training for musicians to provide music therapy in hospitals: the Music Educators National Conference, the Music Teacher's National Association (MTNA), and the Music Industry Council.

On June 2, 1950, the committee of the MTNA held a meeting to draft bylaws to set up a new organization devoted to music therapy. Ray Green became the first president of the newly formed National Association for Music Therapy (NAMT), the first association created for this purpose—not only in this country but also in the entire world.

As Hunter stated, "So the starting date of the profession of music therapy is June 2, 1950. Over the next fifty years there was continuous growth in what I think of as the newest and certainly one of the oldest healing therapies in human civilization."

In 1971 a second association was established, the American Association for Music Therapy (AAMT), originally called the Urban Federation of Music Therapists. Many of the purposes of AAMT were similar to those of NAMT, but some policies and procedures differed on education, clinical training, and certification.

The Certification Board for Music Therapists was established in 1983 to provide a nationally recognized credential available to all music therapists. To date, over six thousand music therapists maintain the MT-BC credential (Music Therapist-Board Certified).

The American Music Therapy Association was formed in 1998 from the unification of the National Association for Music Therapy and the American Association for Music Therapy. It is the single largest music therapy association in the world.

By now I felt much more a part of a very big picture. I'd left the cocoon of the SICU in one respect, as I knew that I was involved in a huge piece of human history. I felt honored to be a part of the Louis Armstrong Center for Music and Medicine.

Founded in 2005, this center is an umbrella organization directed by Dr. Loewy. It includes the music therapy department at Mount Sinai Beth Israel and is also involved in research projects and ongoing programs, with a wide range of interdisciplinary teams that include doctors, nurses, social workers, physical therapists, and other health care professionals.

Armstrong died on July 6, 1971. Over the last years of his life, he was a patient at Beth Israel Medical Center and developed a love for the place. He stated, "My doctor—he saved my life at the Beth Israel Hospital, N.Y. Dr. Zucker took me out of intensive care. Twice. Yea." Before he died, he said, "I want to give back some of the goodness I received." His desire to give back, by making a donation from his foundation to set up a music therapy department, came out of his own experience of being saved at Beth Israel.

When Armstrong was a patient there in 1969, with a rapidly deteriorating heart condition, his lungs filled with fluid and he had to undergo an emergency tracheotomy to clear them. Anxiety set in postsurgery and Armstrong's cheerful disposition changed dramatically as he spiraled into introspection and despondence, thoughts of death, and a reassessment of his life and career.

His doctor, Dr. Gary Zucker, noticing his depressive state, sang a simple song to his patient, a lullaby brought to the United States by Jewish immigrants from Eastern Europe. On hearing it, Armstrong brightened. It turned out to be a song from his childhood, one that he'd sung along with members of a Jewish family in New Orleans, the Karnofskys, who had given him odd jobs and cared for him. The lullaby seemed to pull him out of his deep depression and galvanize him. Almost immediately, Armstrong began to write a memoir of his childhood and coming of age in the South.

When one of the greatest musicians of all time was slipping away, a doctor who understood the power of music to heal pulled him back from the precipice by singing to him, and Armstrong knew that he couldn't thank God enough, or his doctors, or his loved ones. To give thanks, you have to give something. In doing so, he gave thanks for all the many gifts of his lifetime. And created something of enduring value, as enduring as the music he made that will be in the hearts of so many of us, forever.

Boethius,* an influential authority on music in the early Middle Ages, strongly emphasized the influence of music on a person's character and moral and ethical behavior.

Like the Greeks, Boethius regarded music as a "corollary of arithmetic, thus exemplifying in sounds the fundamental principles of order and harmony that prevail throughout the universe."

"Music is so naturally united with us that we cannot be free from it even if we so desired." Boethius, De institutione musica, 1,1,187.9–10

—Jacqueline Schmidt Peters,
Music Therapy: An Introduction

*Anicius Manlius Severinus Boëthius, commonly called Boethius (c. 480–524 AD), was a philosopher of the early sixth century, born in Rome. Boethius entered public life at a young age and was a senator by the age of twenty-five. Boethius was imprisoned and eventually executed by King Theodoric the Great, who suspected him of conspiring with the Byzantine Empire. While jailed, Boethius composed his Consolation of Philosophy, which became one of the most popular and influential works of the Middle Ages.

8

Alice Blue Gown

I WOULD TELL Wendy there were two kinds of days in the SICU: ordinary and extraordinary. The ordinary days were fine— nothing dramatic happened but most everybody felt a little better having music fill the air. Those were the days when I'd suddenly break into "Here Comes the Sun" for Dr. McMillen. His favorite. The extraordinary days, though, were the kind you never forget. By the end of my first six months, which coincided with the first anniversary of my surgery and coma, I'd probably had more extraordinary days than in all the years of my life before that.

At one point, Wendy wondered whether I might cut back from three days in the SICU to two. Money was tight, and it would have been a rational decision, but I vehemently refused, outraged by the idea. I hadn't realized I felt so passionate about my days at the hospital, but I saw now that my work there was so energizing to me, so life affirming, that it had become essential.

Galina Mindlin, M.D., Columbia University professor of psychiatry, believes that music is built into the human cells, especially brain cells, from the hour of conception. In her book *Your Playlist Can Change Your Life,* she states, "The first music encoded deep within your memory are the earliest vibrations that made you—the rhythms and tempos of your first cells. As your cells began to develop with the comforting rhythms of your mother's heartbeat and the whooshing low frequency sounds vibrating through her placenta and your umbilical cord, these first musical scores began entrainment (two or more rhythms synchronizing into one) in your brain and orchestrating the essence of music for your entire being. So from your first spark of life, your brain was already establishing the relationship for how music affects you today."

The morning I was born at St. Joseph's Hospital in Far Rockaway, New York, my Grandma Molly went to the nursery to see me before she went upstairs to see my mother. She decided that I was such an ugly baby, with a full head of curly black hair and a pushed-in nose, that I couldn't be one of her progeny. Molly insisted on an investigation to make sure there hadn't been a baby switch. When she went up to see my mother she had the Mother Superior, this being a Catholic hospital, with her, none too pleased at the moment, and they actually checked the paperwork at the doctor's office to see whether I was the real baby. I was.

The story had become a perennial, laughed over at holiday dinners, but one day when I was fifteen my cousin Miriam told me more about that day. Standing over me, with voice lowered, she said, "I was there that morning. I saw you in the nursery. There were four nurses, wearing those old-fashioned white uniforms with the white caps. They knew about the baby-switch investigation and they'd felt sorry for you. Not only had they put a blue ribbon in your hair, but they sang to you all morning as well. Show tunes, I heard them when I was there. It was so lovely." She looked off into the distance, lost in the memory, then someone called her, she walked away, and the moment was over. But it was enough.

I like to think that my brain was wired in the nursery by the healing power of music.

On my way in one Monday afternoon, I noticed a patient in Bed 6, a woman of about sixty, wearing a pale-blue hospital gown. Her long reddish hair on the left side of her head was starting to gray, but the right side was shaved. A sign, I knew by now, that she'd had brain surgery. Her pale skin was waxy looking, her eyes were swollen shut, and she was intubated. The ventilator hummed on the right side of the bed, while on the left stood a strange-looking machine attached to her head by a long thin line. It turned out to be an ICP (intracranial pressure) machine to monitor the pressure inside her skull, brain tissue, and cerebrospinal fluid. Taped to the back wall was a sign that said "Don't Touch Cranium." Her vital signs on the computer monitor didn't seem too bad—on the high side, but still within the normal range. But this woman was far from being in good health.

At home, I'd recently played an old tune called "Alice Blue

Gown," a 1919 hit inspired by Alice Roosevelt Longworth, daughter of Theodore Roosevelt. Looking at this woman in her hospital gown as I set up my guitar, the words "Alice Blue Gown" popped into my head. I would give her this name as she couldn't communicate her own to me.

By this time, I had Dr. McMillen's approval to start making my own decisions about which bedsides to go to and in what order. My instinct now was that Alice needed music the most.

I took out my Bach folder. Since my experience with the "Russian woman" with misfiring nerve synapses, I always went for Bach first for patients recovering from brain surgery. In these instances, I kept in mind neuromusicologist Arthur Harvey's quote that Bach's music helped the "brain work in a balanced way" more than any other music.

I started to quietly tune my guitar and then played a chord. Usually I saw a reaction at a patient's bedside to the first sounds of the guitar, even in someone heavily sedated or in a coma. Typically, there is some movement in the face, even if just a twitch or two. As I knew well, it is a medical fact that hearing is the last sense to go—the auditory nerve functions until the very end. However, I could see no discernible reaction at all from Alice. Not on her face, no movement in her hands or legs. Nothing. I could barely even see her breathing. She hardly seemed to be alive.

I started playing a well-known chorale from a Bach cantata, Sleepers Awake, music with a particularly graceful melody and flowing rhythm. Even though I was reading from the music on my stand, I glanced up quickly and often at Alice's face, hands, and feet to see if there was any change. This was a skill I'd developed over the past few months. I was especially looking for signs of agitation, which could mean the music wasn't helping. I also glanced up at the monitor as often as I could. Her heart rate and blood pressure had both lowered a little. But I saw nothing different in her appearance. I couldn't recall ever playing for someone who seemed so not there. It was as if there was no one home. A very disconcerting feeling. I took out more music, more Bach, and settled in. She was by far the sickest person there that day. I decided to spend my whole session with her.

As I played, my eyes moved from the sheet music to Alice's face to the computer monitors and back again. Her chest rose and fell as the ventilator hummed next to her, but there was no sign of life in her face or anywhere. There was no sense of soul. I was suddenly aware that this is what I must have looked like in my coma. Lying in the bed, looking so deeply asleep, so far away. Had I, too, looked as if there was no one home? Alice's face gave no indication of thought of any kind, and yet maybe she was having the same vivid dreams that I'd had. It was hard to imagine that her brain could be flooded with the visions I'd seen, continuous larger-than-life sequences that pounded through my mind as I slept, completely unresponsive. It didn't look like there was any brain activity at all.

After an hour, I stopped to stretch, then turned in my chair to see what was happening at the other end of the unit. I was startled to hear a sound. Like a gasp for breath. I looked back. It was Alice. Her eyes were still tightly shut but she gasped again. Then again, and her face reddened slightly. She seemed agitated.

I looked up at the computer monitor. Her heart rate and blood pressure were going up fast. Alarmingly fast. Her heart was racing. My heart started racing, too.

The two nurses behind the Nurses' Station didn't seem to have noticed. It's a very tricky thing for the musician to get involved in something like this so I hesitated. But then I saw an intern sitting at a computer about six feet away and asked him if Alice needed attention.

He turned to look at her and the computer screen above, frowned, then rubbed his hand against the stubble on his chin. "It's okay. She sometimes has episodes like this."

I asked him exactly what her medical situation was. There are patient privacy laws, but Dr. McMillen had told everyone I was to be considered part of the staff and could be briefed on specifics.

"She suffered a massive hemorrhagic stroke and had surgery to relieve the pressure on her brain from fluid buildup. Some strokes are caused by the brain getting too much blood, some by the brain not getting enough. This was the first kind." He turned back to look at Alice and shook his head slightly.

I nodded. "When I started playing, her heart rate and blood pressure lowered. It was like that for an hour. The minute I stopped playing, everything shot up again. Could that have been a reaction to the music stopping?"

"I don't know, but it's possible."

"Should I keep playing for her?"

He shrugged. "It certainly couldn't hurt. We want to see her blood pressure come down so you're helping with that." He paused for a moment. "We work under the assumption that she has at least *some* neurological function, so she might be hearing the music on some level. We just don't know." He turned back to his computer.

I went back to Alice, sat down, and started playing. For the next few minutes, I looked at the music, then up at the computer screen, and back again. Within minutes, her vital signs were back down to where they had been before. I couldn't be sure if it was because of the music, but at least she was moving in the right direction. I decided to stay longer than usual.

There's something in music therapy called entrainment. It's a term from physics that explains that two objects moving together use less energy than two objects moving in opposite directions; so, if they are placed next to each other, they will, eventually, begin to move together in synchronicity. For example, one pendulum will begin swinging at the same rate as the one next to it. In other words, entrainment is the tendency of two oscillating bodies to lock into phase, so they vibrate in sympathetic harmony. Our internal rhythms—heart rate and respiration rate—will speed up or slow down to match a stronger external rhythm such as waves lapping a beach or speeding traffic. Or the incessant pulsing noise of machines and television and talking in a SICU. Most patients' vital signs are higher than normal in such an environment. Music can reach out to a patient to get in synch and balance any disharmony. I tried that with Alice now, trying to find a way to reach her, to have the music resonate within her.

Finally, it reached the point when I had to return home, so I thought about the best music to leave her with. I took out the fugue from Bach's Prelude, Fugue, and Allegro. A few weeks earlier, I'd played it for a patient in a coma and one of the nurses who was particularly interested in music sat with me and listened all the way through. We both saw a significant improvement in the patient's vital signs by the conclusion of the piece. When I asked the nurse why it seemed to have such a strong effect, she closed her eyes for a second and said, "It sounds like life itself." I thought it might work for Alice.

This fugue starts off with a simple and inviting opening melody that gradually increases in complexity and expands with subtle modulations all kept together by a steady walking tempo. I wanted to pull Alice along on a journey into beauty and wonder, away from pain and worry.

One of my music professors in college—Bülent Arel, a brilliant, funny, Turkish-born composer—once said very seriously, "The music must never leave the song and the dance, or it is not music anymore." From then on, whenever playing the guitar, I imagine the melody coming from singers on stage and in costume, and costumed dancers flowing to the rhythm. Every piece becomes the sound track to a scene in a movie and tells a story, and in the telling of a musical story I fully engage every part of myself. This was how I played for Alice now—with all of myself.

At the majestic final cadence of the fugue, I paused to let the notes spin out from my guitar and linger until they faded away into nothingness. I waited another few moments and then stood up. Though her vital signs were better now than when I'd started playing, she didn't look different in any way. On an impulse, I leaned forward and whispered, "Did you like the music, Alice?"

Within a split second, two loud beeps sounded—I couldn't tell from where but they got my attention. There hadn't been a single sign of life from her other than the gasps I'd heard earlier.

I watched for a few more seconds. She didn't move or make a sound. I went to pack up my guitar.

On my way to the exit, I walked past Bed 6 again and saw a nurse entering data into Alice's chart. It was Rosievic.

"Rosie, I played my whole session today at Alice's bedside, and I have a question for you. When I finished playing, I leaned over and asked her if she'd liked the music, and I immediately heard two loud beeps. Could that have been some kind of response from her?"

Rosie is not only a consummate professional; she always gets right to the point.

"Well, let's find out." She went to Alice, took her right hand, and in a loud clear voice said, "Alice, it's Monday at five P.M. If you heard the music, I want you to squeeze my hand." We both watched. I was holding my breath. Nothing. Then Rosievic said again, slowly, "Alice, if you heard the music, squeeze my hand."

No response. Alice didn't move. There was nothing but the hum of the ventilator machine.

I knew I'd just learned the most crucial lesson yet, maybe the most crucial lesson I'd ever learn. Hearing those beeps and thinking my music had gotten through to a severely damaged patient raised my hopes and was simply unrealistic. I had to remind myself that rule no. 3 was as important to me now as it had been when I was a patient: be completely reality based. I needed to respond to the facts of what was happening to the patient instead of my hopes about what *might* happen. Otherwise the emotional ups and downs would wear me out.

Another few seconds went by, and then, just as I was about to turn away, I saw something. Almost imperceptibly, Alice's fingers started to move. Twenty seconds, maybe more, had gone by since Rosievic had asked Alice the question. But there was no doubt, all of a sudden, that she started to squeeze Rosievic's hand. Her fingers tightened ever so slightly, more and more. Rosievic and I both looked up, our eyes meeting, wide with surprise. And hope.

"Rosie, do you think that's real, or could it just be a reflex?"

She turned back to her patient and said, again slowly and clearly, "Alice, our guitarist will be here again on Wednesday. If you want to hear the music then, give me a thumbs-up."

We stared at Alice's hand, and again it seemed like an eternity as the seconds passed. Rosie was holding her breath this time, as well. And then, there it was—very slowly, and with what must have been enormous effort, her hand began to tremble and then started slowly rotating to the right.

Thumbs-up. Thumbs-up! Wow!

It was an astonishing moment. I was so happy I could barely contain myself. I moved in closer and said, "Alice, I'm Andrew, your guitarist, I will see you again on Wednesday. I'll play more music for you. Feel better!" As I walked out of the SICU I had a new understanding of the resilience of the human body and spirit. That was the real lesson, and one never to be forgotten. From that moment on I have *always* assumed that there is someone home, no matter how critically ill the patient is. There is really no point in being there otherwise.

Two days later, when I arrived back in the SICU, Alice was still in Bed 6, now sleeping comfortably. The ICP machine was gone. I asked one of the nurses why it had been moved. She smiled, shrugged, and said, "She doesn't need it anymore." A moment later,

I saw a neurologist head over to Bed 6, look at the patient and the chart, and ask another doctor to come over. Still looking at the chart, she shook her head and said, "She's doing much better, and we don't know why."

I smiled, and after a few moments started playing some Bach.

I knew that the music had somehow reached Alice Blue Gown, that she had processed it, and been able to respond to it. She had shown us that she was still home. But, I didn't know how. What was happening inside Alice's brain while she listened to the music?

I know my limits. So when I want to know what's going on from the perspective of neuroscience, I ask the experts. Dr. Kamran Fallahpour is a clinical psychologist and neuroscientist, the founder and director of the Brain Resource Center in New York City. Fallahpour focuses on neuroenhancement interventions that guide brain plasticity and help retrain the brain for enhanced brain health, better cognitive skills, and improved self-regulation.

My question for Fallahpour was how was Alice able to give a thumbs-up after hearing music when no one thought she had the neurologic function left to do that.

"Well, Alice had a severe disorder of consciousness," he said. "In such cases, damage is seldom restricted to one area. Often these patients have suffered a global brain dysfunction involving the brain stem following some form of severe traumatic brain injury—in Alice's case, a stroke followed by brain surgery. Patients with these disorders may flow in and out of various stages of consciousness during their recovery, so first we need to consider the possible state that Alice was in while the music was playing. A coma, a vegetative state, or a minimally conscious state. Coma is described as an absence of arousal and awareness.

"In the case of a vegetative state, there is not a complete lack of arousal in the brain, but there are still no behavioral signs of awareness. In these patients, the autonomous functions are intact and respiration does not need assistance, but they do not exhibit any particular signs of self-awareness or interest in their environment, and there are still no voluntary responses or intelligible verbalizations."

A person in a minimally conscious state, a step above the vegetative state in terms of consciousness, can *sometimes* follow simple instructions, communicate yes or no by talking or gesturing, speak understandable words, and respond to people, things, or events with facial expressions, sounds, and gestures.

But, as Fallahpour explained, "In such patients, though there is evidence of arousal and also some discernible signs of awareness, such signs may be fleeting or inconsistent. As a vegetative patient's levels of awareness and consciousness improve, he or she may enter into the minimally conscious state. It is often difficult to discern a patient's exact level of consciousness, and as a result, misdiagnoses are common."

In Alice's case, her doctors had presumed some level of neurological function but it was very hard to tell, given her seeming lack of awareness. She could have been fluctuating between states of consciousness without anyone noticing until Rosie and I interacted with her.

"One of the questions we have," continued Fallahpour, "is how much cognitive function a person has in these states and how can we find out? We know that brain regions such as the brain stem (arousal), the amygdala (emotions), and the cerebellum (motor control and sense of rhythm) can respond to sound and music even when the patient is in a semivegetative state with no conscious awareness. When you played music to Alice for a very long time it is likely that these regions of her brain were processing the sound. After you whispered, 'Did you like the music, Alice?' two loud beeps sounded. It is very likely that the beeps were related to physiological changes in Alice's brain and nervous system. She was responding not only to the music, but also to your comment, and so processing both music and language. What happened next was that Rosievic asked Alice for a response or a sign, and then came the hand squeeze and the thumbs-up."

Alice's hand movements were further evidence that she was not only neurologically intact, but that she had moved into a minimally conscious state—able to direct her responses and communicate with Rosie and me.

"It is likely that the music you played stimulated these different areas of the brain, thereby connecting her more concretely to her external environment and encouraging a more conscious state of awareness; as her levels of awareness increased, she was better able to respond to Rosievic, albeit gradually. The timing of this process may have been a considerable factor. If the music or the comment were made a few minutes earlier or later, she may have not responded at all! Music and sound have a primary and direct gateway to our state of arousal and consciousness."

This was music to my ears.

Fallahpour confirmed, "In Alice's case, it's likely that the music stimulated the brain stem, which in turn stimulated the cortex, then the brain was more aroused and speech was processed by both Alice's auditory cortex and then higher areas of her brain such as the frontal lobe, which helps with interpretation and meaning, allowing her to comprehend the question and act upon it.

"However, it is also likely that it took a massive effort and a slow reaction time to get various brain regions such as the prefrontal lobe and the motor areas sufficiently online to be able to conceive of, coordinate, and execute even such a simple response as a thumbs-up. At such low levels of arousal and awareness, making sense of the request may have been as difficult as trying to spot a ship on a foggy horizon after major eye surgery.

"In addition, it is interesting to consider whether Alice would have responded in a similar manner had you played anything other than Bach, or even that specific fugue. We will never know. However, it is certainly conceivable that the neurologically stimulating nature of Bach's fugal structure, symmetry, and complexity played an important role in getting Alice to the point where she was able to come out of the vegetative state and enter the minimally conscious state and be able to process, comprehend, and respond as she did."

What Rosie and I saw, and what Fallahpour explained, reinforced how I felt that day after Alice's thumbs-up. Always assume someone is home. And the power of music to get through to the patient can be the key that opens the door.

I couldn't stop thinking about Fallahpour's comment that misdiagnoses are common in determining a patient's state of consciousness as it can be extremely difficult for doctors to differentiate between states. There are accepted diagnostic criteria used by doctors for each condition but it is still easy to miss important signs and so diagnose a minimally conscious patient as vegetative. The differences in care, and medical outcome, for someone in a vegetative state versus someone in a minimally conscious state are huge. Minimally conscious patients have a much better chance of recovery.

With advances in neuroimaging, there is now the possibility of stimulating the brain as part of the diagnostic procedure—for example, by showing a family photo or touching or talking to the patient—and measuring any corresponding brain activity through changes in blood flow with functional MRI technology (fMRI), or by measuring glucose metabolism with PET scans. This should make misdiagnosis much less likely.

British neuroscientist Adrian Owen, whose research paper on diagnosis of vegetative states appeared in *Science* in 2006, has stated that "close to 20 percent of patients who are thought to be vegetative are actually conscious, but are nevertheless incapable of demonstrating their consciousness through standard clinical assessments. To date only fMRI has proven itself to be a reliable method for identifying such 'covert consciousness' in this unusual population of patients, although we and other groups are working to see whether electrophysiological methods can be used for the same purpose." His paper reported on the brain function of a twenty-three-year-old woman left in a vegetative state after a car crash. During an fMRI scan of her brain he asked her to imagine playing tennis and noted her response: the supplementary motor cortex lit up, just as in the brains of healthy volunteers. She was clearly not in a vegetative state despite her diagnosis.

Fallahpour suggested that an EEG (electroencephalography) and qEEG (quantitative electroencephalography—often thought of as brain mapping) of a patient in a coma could be of prognostic value as to whether a patient would recover. He explained, "Certain brain activity patterns can be observed in those coma patients more likely to move from coma to vegetative state and minimally conscious state, and eventually become fully conscious. A spindle coma pattern is a good example of this, whereas other patterns of brain activity—such as burst suppression and alpha-theta coma—represent a poor prognosis and less likelihood of a patient improving into higher levels of arousal and consciousness. Of course, there can always be exceptions."

This reinforced what I had quickly learned as a critical care musician: there are always exceptions and you have to be constantly vigilant.

It had really hit home for me that day how sick I had been. Of course, I'd known on a rational level that my survival was a miracle, but seeing Alice in an unconscious state, possibly drifting between levels of arousal and awareness, made me realize how far from myself I had gone, how out of sync and unbalanced I must have been.

Part of me was convinced that Alice was in a vegetative state, neurologically gone, as I played for her. I had never before seen a SICU patient as unresponsive as she. It would have been easy to dismiss her and move on to the next patient, one who showed more signs of life. I was relieved that I hadn't.

Given Alice's astonishing response, and Fallahpour's confirmation of the role the music might have played in stimulating her brain and showing us that many regions of her brain were functioning, perhaps music could be used as a diagnostic tool in the future. It could be a way of letting the patient say, "I'm still here. There's somebody home."

Thinking back later about Alice Blue Gown, I was awed once again by the idea that that was what I had looked like in the coma, so unreachable, locked in my own state of consciousness, disordered and dysfunctional. I could visualize what Wendy had seen, what the medical staff had seen, and I appreciated again Wendy's inspiration that something inside me was broken, out of sync, and could perhaps be reached—and helped—by music. As with Alice, there was no other clear way to get through.

I pictured myself lying in Bed 7 in a coma, with an earbud attached to an iPod in one ear. Next to me, Wendy pressed the first track and the *St. Matthew Passion* started to play. I truly believe the complex vibration of my favorite piece of music caused me to vibrate in sympathetic response on the most fundamental level. Even in a coma, my body and brain—perhaps even my soul—had locked on to the music, entrained to it, and helped pull me back to consciousness.

It wasn't a surprise, then, for me to learn that research studies show that music is strongly associated with the brain's reward system—the region of the brain that tells us if something is important or has a survival value. When we listen to music, especially music that is pleasurable to us to the extent it sends shivers down the spine, activity is triggered in the nucleus accumbens, the part of the brain that releases the chemical dopamine. This feel-good hormone is also released in response to food or sex, evolutionarily important activities.

I like to think that my brain entrained to its beloved *St. Matthew Passion* and responded with a tenacious need to survive.

During the Middle Ages, a peculiar malady known as tarantism arose, particularly prevalent in Italy.

This disease, believed to be caused by the sting of the tarantula, was characterized by alternating fits of frenzy and complete inertia.

Treatment and catharsis were achieved only through music and dancing. In order to effect a cure, musicians had to be able to match the music to the symptoms of the patient.

The curative tarantellas would mirror the tempi and movements appropriate to the particular type of spider that had bitten and taken possession of the afflicted individual and then change to show the return of the patient's identity and the fight against the spider's possession.

—Jacqueline Schmidt Peters,
Music Therapy: An Introduction

9

Better Than a Standing Ovation

It was the last day of my first year of playing in the SICU, January 19, 2011, and I was feeling exceptionally good. I was walking through Stuyvesant Square for the umpteenth time but it was anything but boring. It had been a fantastic year of learning about being a medical musician, my health was very good, and the square always reminded me of Wendy. I almost did a little dance as I passed through the front door of Beth Israel Medical Center.

That day, there was a new patient in Bed 7. He was either sleeping or sedated. A man about my age, late fifties, eyes closed tight, his face drawn, pale, and haggard. Standing next to his bed was an exceptionally attractive woman, about fifty, dressed in casual but expensive-looking clothing. She appeared anxious, caressing his face with her hands and talking softly.

One of the nurses assigned to Bed 7 came over to me. "This patient has pancreatic cancer. The surgery was two days ago. He's heavily sedated, and doing very poorly. I told his wife your story, and she asked if you would play for him."

For a moment, I closed my eyes and just sat. Not so long ago, I'd awoken in that same bed thinking I had pancreatic cancer. I remembered the fear that had coursed through my mind and body, and was probably flooding through the patient now. I glanced at his wife leaning over and caring for him. That might easily have been Wendy doing the same for me. I would do my best to help now at Bed 7.

When I arrived at her husband's bedside the woman looked up and smiled broadly. "The nurse told me you had pancreatic cancer." She'd obviously misunderstood what the nurse had said—or perhaps heard what she wanted to hear. I gave her a short account of what happened to me while she listened intently, and then I began. Bach's Prelude from the *First Cello Suite*, the piece I had played for Dr. Loewy the first time I met her and for so many patients since my return, music that had always proved to be exceptionally soothing and healing. Once again, it worked its magic. Within a few seconds there was a movement at the patient's right side. It was his hand. The music had gotten through immediately. He began to move his fingers and then very slowly began to raise his hand, bending from the wrist.

His wife and I turned to each other, beaming smiles, eyes widening. I felt sure that we were sharing the same thought: "Amazing! The power of music!"

I looked back at her husband's face. In an instant, I knew something was wrong. Very wrong. She did, too. The slight movement of his fingers grew more rapid, his wrist rose slightly, palm bending back, as if he were pushing against something. With tremendous effort, he began to raise his arm. His wife leaned forward. "Honey, do you want the music to stop?" Eyes still closed, he tilted his head forward a few inches, back, and forward again. A nod.

I was shocked. This had never happened before, a patient asking me to stop playing. Certainly, there were times when patients or family members were asked if they wanted music at the bedside and said no. On a few occasions, someone had asked me to play in a different spot because a patient had a bad headache. But never something like this.

So as not to make things worse by suddenly cutting off the sound, I faded out over the next few seconds. The woman looked upset, but in another moment I realized she was not upset with me. Turning toward me, she whispered, "I'm so sorry."

Amazed by her concern for me in that moment, I whispered, "I understand," and slipped away.

Later, as I walked through Stuyvesant Square on my way to the Union Square subway, I felt like kicking myself. I was certain I knew what had happened. I should have been much more aware, for if there's anyone who should know that a patient can hear things when sedated, even when in a coma, it's me.

As he lay there, after surgery for pancreatic cancer, the patient must have heard me regaling his wife with how I had been so fortunate as to *not* have pancreatic cancer, how I had survived anaphylactic shock, and even clinical death. And now here I was, alive and well and back in the SICU. It could only sound to him as if I was charming his wife with the tale of my medical miracle. I could guess what was going on in his mind when he lifted his hand and started moving it with such urgency.

"Oh, you didn't have cancer and you were too strong to die. How *nice* for you. And now you're hitting on my beautiful wife with this marvelous story? Well, listen, buddy, I DO have cancer and I'm probably going to die, and you and your guitar can go *fuck off*. Get out of here. Leave!"

I was mortified by my lack of sensitivity in the situation, by how I'd made the patient feel. What an awful mistake. I'd caused agitation or worse to a patient. The exact opposite of soothing and healing. If I'd just been thinking and acting properly, about why I was there and whom I was playing for, instead of feeling so self-satisfied about my accomplishments of the past year, I could have helped this guy.

As I crossed Second Avenue, I realized this is the stress the medical staff have to live with every day. Years of perfect work can be ruined by one disastrous mistake. Putting a decimal point in the wrong place when filling a prescription, inserting a line in the wrong vein, so many things that can go wrong and create a bad, even fatal, response. At the same time, I knew I couldn't let a mistake paralyze me. I had to learn from it, let it go, and move forward. Keep it in perspective. A thought flashed through my mind, about that old rule I'd used when I was a patient—to make my doctors and nurses laugh as much as possible. Next thought:

I'd never heard of a classical guitarist being sued for medical malpractice.

It worked. I laughed. I let it go.

Two days later, I was back in the SICU. It was the first day of my second year. The patient in Bed 7 was alone, his eyes still closed, face paler, cheeks hollowing. Walking behind the Nurses' Station, I took my guitar out of its case and asked how he was doing. A physician's assistant grimaced and shook his head. "He's very sick, doesn't look good."

Bed 7 was so close to my central spot that, for a few moments, I considered going to the other end of the unit. Then I remembered a rehearsal with my string quintet when one of the players flubbed a passage but got it perfect on the repeat. She looked up and said, "God created repeats so you get a second chance!" I wanted a repeat, a second chance, too. I sat down and began to play but for the first few minutes I made sure to keep my eyes focused like a hawk on the patient's right hand. No movement. I relaxed a bit and stayed put.

After twenty minutes of playing, I decided to go over to the bedside, pull up a chair, and settle in. I started with the same Bach prelude again, very slowly, and very carefully watching the patient's pale face, his hand. I was actually curious—maybe he just didn't like Bach? Sometimes a piece of music can have negative connotations—I'd seen it before. The seconds ticked by; no hand movements. After a few minutes, I relaxed and continued playing the other movements that followed the prelude, all dance movements in different tempos, and all elegant and lyrical. When I finished the suite, I looked up at his vital signs monitor. His heart rate was 125 and his blood pressure was 149 over 79. The blood pressure was a little high yet not above the high end of normal, but a heart rate of 125 in someone this sick was very concerning. After fifteen more minutes, some slow Spanish pieces, I cautiously looked up again at the monitor. Still no change in either number. I had *always* been able to lower heart rate and blood pressure with this music.

I *swore* to myself that I wouldn't look up at the monitor again and sat back, relaxed, and played straight from the heart. In a way, I was playing for both of us.

Although most people thought of me as a "former" patient who'd returned to the SICU to give back, I was, and will always be, a *patient*. I have what is rather unpoetically referred to as "unspecified pancreas disease." That's what my medical chart says. It means I will always have the potential to develop pancreatic cancer. I have a cyst in my pancreas still. Its removal would mean the complete removal of my pancreas so instead we continue to monitor it, even as it grows. I'm completely aware that it could turn cancerous, that at any moment I could end up in the SICU again, back on the other side of the curtain.

I let the music pour out of my guitar. "Here Comes the Sun" by George Harrison, Luiz Bonfá's "Manhã de Carnaval" from the film *Black Orpheus*, "Summertime" and more by the Gershwins, more Bach. I lost myself in pure musical feeling and left behind the swirling thoughts of whether or not I could heal him. I entered a state of flow, what many musicians call being in the zone—so fully immersed in your playing that nothing else exists.

Half an hour went by. I couldn't resist returning to the reality of the SICU, the here and now of what was happening with this patient. I'd sworn to myself I wouldn't look at the monitor again. I couldn't help myself. I looked up at the screen.

To my utter astonishment, his heart rate was 105 and his blood pressure was 122/74 and, even more important, his face had color. It was no longer a slate of gray. A huge improvement.

I could barely contain myself. "Penny," I whispered to the nurse filling in his chart. "Look! 105. He was 125 when I started!" She was the same nurse who'd been there when I played for the old jazz musician, Mr. G. She looked at the monitor and her eyes widened for a moment. Then, turning back to me with her whimsical smile, she said in her lilting Grenadian accent, "Andrew, you don't have to convince *me*." She already knew that music was a healer.

Just at that moment, one of the attending physicians, new to the SICU, Dr. Asaf Gave, walked over to the bed with three medical students in tow. I'd noticed that when he was on rounds he was all business. I'd never seen him smile. But now, looking up at the monitor, he saw the numbers, turned to the medical students, and said in a loud voice, "This guy has *never* been 105!" He motioned to the students to continue on the rounds and, as he passed me, I got an approving nod and smile. It felt like pure gold.

Later, I realized what good doctoring that was. The loud voice was meant for the patient, to give him hope. The nod and smile were for me.

During my career as a concert and club musician, I'd had my

share of compliments from many people, musicians and non-musicians alike, even some standing ovations. But there had never been a moment that meant as much to me as when I looked up and saw that heart rate at 105. I knew then, more than ever before, why I came here three times a week.

Although I couldn't see into this patient's heart and mind, I could look at that computer monitor, see the numbers of his physiological response, and see the color returning to his face, and know unquestionably that he was feeling better.

Most musicians I've met talk about the pleasure they get from giving something to another human being through music. Helping people get through bad times as well as good. Being part of another person's life, being, even if just for a few minutes, the sound track of someone's experience.

Pianist Karl Paulnack delivered a moving testament to the power of music in a 2004 welcome address he gave when he was music division director of the Boston Conservatory. He and a violinist friend were putting on a concert in a nursing home in a small Midwestern town. They began with Aaron Copland's Sonata, music dedicated to a young pilot, a friend of Copland's, who was shot down during World War II. Partway through the piece, an elderly man, clearly a soldier, began to weep, and later, when Paulnack explained the circumstances behind the music, he left the room. It turned out that he, too, had been a pilot in World War II and had seen a friend shot down and plummet into the ocean. He hadn't thought about that memory for years, yet Copland's Sonata brought it back to him so vividly that it was as if he was reliving it. His questions were, "How does the music do that? How did it find those feelings and those memories in me?" Paulnack stated that the concert in the nursing home was the most important work he had ever done.

I felt exactly the same way about playing for the patient in Bed 7.

As I packed up to leave, I hoped this man would get through this. As happens in so many cases, I'd never know. I never saw him again; he'd been moved to Step-Down the next time I returned, and I never heard any follow-up, even though I asked.

I hope he's reading this right now.

During the Middle Ages, the Greek and Roman traditions of philosophy, music and medicine were preserved in the Arab culture which was at its height in the 8th and 9th centuries. Works of Greek physicians and philosophers were translated into Arabic, and the idea that musical regularity was related to universal order and relations was an integral part of Arab thought. In hospitals in Cairo, music was played on the wards, with human voices or stringed instruments.

—Jacqueline Schmidt Peters,
Music Therapy: An Introduction

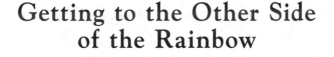

10

Getting to the Other Side
of the Rainbow

I HAD THOUGHT of my father the day before, just as I did every
June 6, the anniversary of D-Day. If it hadn't been for the jammed
thumb from the baseball game, he might well have landed on
Omaha Beach and I might have remained a figment of my
mother's imagination. I'd remembered the music he loved—the
Big Band music of the '30s and '40s, all those great American
standards like "In the Mood" and "Begin the Beguine," many of
which I'd arranged for guitar. In his honor, today my black bag
contained the folder marked THE GREAT AMERICAN SONGBOOK.

In the last few weeks, I'd started something new when I arrived
at the SICU. I called it the Dr. Sarah Edwards Promenade. One
of the young doctors, Edwards, had suggested that at the beginning of each session, after tuning my guitar, consulting the main
computer monitor behind the Nurses' Station for several minutes,
and checking all the vital signs for each patient very carefully,

I should take a stroll through the unit. I'd play a soothing piece while walking by, see all the patients up close, and let them see and hear me. That way I could decide where best to direct my music and at the same time give each patient a chance to make a decision as to whether they wanted music at their bedside. Once I'd made a complete pass through the unit comparing the vital signs I'd seen at the main monitor with my appraisal of the patient's outward appearance, I'd have done my own form of triage, seeing who needed me most. Once the promenade was complete, I'd usually know the two or three bedsides I'd go to first.

Today, I could see there was something terribly wrong with the patient in Bed 6. The woman—jet-black hair, fair skinned, middle aged—seemed to be in more pain than anybody I'd ever seen in the eighteen months I'd been playing here. I'd come to understand that virtually everyone in a SICU is in some degree of pain—you are only there because you've had major surgery, after all—but there was another dimension here to what I was seeing and hearing. Interestingly, the patient's vital signs were not bad, heart rate and blood pressure a little high, but it reminded me of the constant need to gather and assess as much information as possible.

A constant grimace contorted the patient's face, and her squinting eyes and restless hand and arm movements were further evidence of her severe pain. She reminded me of a child who'd just hurt herself and needed help but could no longer express herself in words. Just the physical language of pain. She was clearly at another level of distress. She swung her head from side to side and, as I watched her, it became obvious that she was talking quietly, then listening, to people visible only to her. She was hallucinating. Talk, listen—talk, listen. "Do anything you want to me," she said suddenly. "Just don't hurt my son." That was followed by silence for a few seconds as she tilted her head to one side, listened to her invisible interlocutor, and calmed down for a minute or so. That didn't last long. Soon she became just as distressed again, and the talk-listen pattern resumed.

The nurse standing nearby, Rosievic Hamilton, saw me watching intently and sensed that I didn't understand what was going on. She explained that the woman was suffering from ICU Delirium, a condition that is a growing concern in modern critical care units. It can be brought on by a number of factors, such as sensory deprivation as patients are in windowless rooms away from family and friends, sleep disturbance, continuous light levels, stress, constant medical monitoring, and noise from medical machines. I could certainly understand.

Two years earlier, the patient had undergone knee surgery, but recently she had developed an infection in her calf. Her primary care doctor wanted her admitted to the hospital immediately, as a precaution, and it was a good thing he did. Some of the most serious infections occur inside the knee joint where the body's immune system has a difficult time fighting infection. She was now in sepsis shock, a severe response to bacteria or other germs. The infection had entered into the joint space, which is one of the most agonizing experiences a patient can undergo. She was at the high end of the numeric pain rating scale. Zero was "no pain," whereas seven to ten was "severe pain—disabling." Her chart was marked nine. As a result, she was being treated with powerful painkillers and antibiotics. This pain combined with strong drugs and disorientation from admission to the SICU was causing her to have severe anxiety, paranoia, and visual and auditory hallucinations. In short, she was in just about the worst condition possible.

I set up and began to play a short piece, an early-nineteenth-century salon piece intended for intimate settings. It was an étude by Matteo Carcassi—a simple lyrical melody with a rhythm mimicking a bubbling brook. A perfect lullaby. Within seconds, the patient looked straight at me, stopped all movement, and for a moment I thought/hoped that she'd snapped out of her delirium. Unfortunately, within another few seconds she was back to the same anxious behavior, talking again to imaginary people, now on both sides of her bed. When I finished the Carcassi, I tried asking her what music she would like to hear, but she was too far gone, too deep in her imagined world, and she didn't look at me, let alone respond.

One of the silver linings in the cloud of having lost my ability to play from memory was that I always brought a wide range of sheet music into the SICU. On this day, I had an especially large choice. I'd brought along the classical music I often played, Bach, Schubert, and Villa-Lobos, as well as the Great American Songbook—music from the early to mid-twentieth century by George and Ira Gershwin, Cole Porter, Irving Berlin, Richard Rodgers and Oscar Hammerstein II, Harold Arlen and Yip Harburg, Hoagy Carmichael, and other great songwriters who created a treasure trove of melodies and lyrics. "Embraceable You," "Anything Goes," "Always," "My Favorite Things," "Last Night When We Were Young," "Georgia on My Mind," and many other gems. I don't sing them; I've done instrumental arrangements of these songs. (When people ask me if I sing I always say, "Only if I want people to leave the room quickly.")

I started with classical music, but after a few minutes I had a hunch that the old pop standards would be a better fit. There's no explaining those hunches, but for decades now I'd been "playing the room," an old musicians' term for being able to read an audience, and I just went with my gut.

Even so, several times during the afternoon I had the impulse to get up and go to another spot in the room. I wasn't getting a clear signal that the patient wanted the music, but neither was there any indication that she wanted me to leave—no shake of the head or raised hand. It was as if I wasn't there. I wanted to help but just didn't know how best to get through. Wendy had told me of her own feelings of hopelessness as she'd sat at my bedside, trying to communicate but unsure of what to say or do. Of how she'd wanted to walk away sometimes but hadn't. I thought of her now. And, remembering her patience with me, I stayed.

Even after switching the repertoire, the patient didn't look in my direction again during my ninety-minute session. Her vital signs didn't show any real change and her agitated behavior continued throughout.

When it was time for me to go, I stood up and regarded her again. Still no response. She remained in that distant world only she could see. I went behind the Nurses' Station, packed up, and on my way out I looked once more at this woman with whom I just couldn't make a connection. Suddenly, she stopped her agitated movements, turned toward me, and returned my gaze.

Struggling to lift her head up a few inches from the pillow, she whispered one word.

"Marvelous."

Her head fell back. Exhausted.

This came as a huge and very welcome surprise! Finally, a clear signal that the music had reached her through her pain and delirium. I nodded, smiled, mouthed the words, "Thank you," and left.

Returning on Wednesday morning, I went straight to Bed 6. The patient was still there. Her condition was exactly the same: the symptoms of pain, talking to unseen companions, everything I'd observed on Monday, the same signs of ICU Delirium. However, her whispered "marvelous" gave me confidence to play near her again. I decided to stick with the Great American Songbook music. As before, when I started the first few notes of "Bidin' My Time," a Gershwin song, she looked up at me and focused for a few seconds, but then returned to the delirium behavior as I continued to play. This concerned me. If she was still in such a bad way two days later, it could only mean she was in a really serious condition. Rosievic confirmed there had been no notable improvement since my last visit. I doubted that her body and mind could take much more of this.

Then, exactly as before, as I passed her bed on my way out, she caught my eye, lifted her head a few inches, and hoarsely mouthed a word, a different one this time.

"Wonderful."

Her head fell back onto the pillow. Still struggling, still exhausted.

Again, a good sign, but with no notable improvement in her

medical condition, I was worried for her. Sepsis can be life threatening, ultimately leading to the failure of internal organs and even death.

As I walked down the hallway toward the elevator, a thought popped into my head. The word "Wonderful" now added to "Marvelous" made sense, even though the order was reversed. "'S wonderful, 's marvelous" are the opening lyrics of the Gershwins' song "'S Wonderful." It's one of lyricist Ira Gershwin's most ingenious song openers.

Was this the patient's way of letting me know, through the daze of delirium, that the music was getting through? If so, it was incredible. For not only must she have heard the music, but she had recognized it, remembered the lyrics, and been able to tell me a specific word from the lyrics as a way to communicate. This would be even more amazing, given that I had not even played "'S Wonderful" to her, just other Gershwin tunes.

And had I heard her say "marvelous" on Monday and made a subliminal neural connection that made me want to play a lot of Gershwin today? Maybe this was an example on both our parts of the amazing workings of the human brain. Or maybe it was a coincidence.

I returned on Friday. As I approached Bed 6, I felt like pumping the air with my fist and yelling out "Yes!" The patient was still lying in bed with her eyes closed, but none of the ICU Delirium symptoms were there. Her face was drawn and she looked exhausted, but most important, she lay quietly. A man, his shock of white hair complementing her black hair perfectly, sat in a chair next to her bed. Probably her husband.

Walking to the back of the Nurses' Station, a blur of rapid

motion filled the corner of my eye. It was Pilar Baker, the nurse who'd said I had a "Christmas tree" during my coma, with a huge grin on her face. What was she so excited about?

She leaned toward me and, speaking very fast, whispered in my ear. "See that man over at Bed 6? His father wrote the words to 'Over the Rainbow.' How cool is that?"

Fist bump. I knew who wrote those lyrics—the patient's husband was the son of legendary lyricist Yip Harburg, who wrote the song with composer Harold Arlen. I'd played one of their songs, "Last Night When We Were Young," for the patient this week! Pilar's enthusiasm was infectious. Enthusiasm, the only infection welcome in a SICU.

"How's the patient doing?" I asked.

"*Much* better," said Pilar with a smile.

I glanced across at Bed 6 again. "Over the Rainbow," which I often played in the SICU, is one of the most famous songs ever written, known to millions of people all over the world. The lyrics played in my head now, and I remembered the gorgeous rainbow I'd seen two years earlier from a room on the hospital's tenth floor, the day before I returned home after my stay as a patient. It was the most beautiful rainbow I'd ever seen, before or since. Back then, I'd taken it as a good omen that I would survive my ordeal. The patient in Bed 6 had also just now passed through a terrible ordeal.

I improvised a plan on the spot. I walked over to the two of them, quietly introducing myself without letting on that I knew about their relationship to Yip. The patient remained with her eyes closed looking even more drained of color and energy this close, but still much better than before.

The gangly man with the white hair, whose smile and energy seemed more like a twenty-something than an eighty-something, quickly stood up and reached out to shake my hand.

"Hi, I'm Ernie Harburg, and this is my wife, Deena." For a few seconds Deena opened her eyes and seemed to recognize me with a fleeting smile. I turned to Ernie and said, "I'm delighted to see her like this—I played for Deena earlier this week, and I was really concerned about her condition."

Ernie responded, "We thank you so much. Deena has told me what a difference the music made for her."

I was thrilled to hear that and told them so.

"I really should start playing now. There's a song I want to start with that I think you both might recognize."

I headed back to my guitar and stand, and began. As soon as I played the instantly recognizable melody, the octave leap on the word "Some-where," Ernie, grinning from ear to ear, was at my side soaking up the music he'd known so intimately for a lifetime. We both saw Deena pull herself up on her pillows, eyes opening wide, a deep smile spreading across her face. It was like watching someone holding a watering can over a wilted flower and seeing it come back to life.

As I finished playing, Deena pushed farther up on her elbows, color in her cheeks now, and exclaimed, "Lovely!" Then she lay back and closed her eyes, but the transformation was complete. She was back. I continued playing, going right into the Gershwins' "Someone to Watch Over Me."

Over the next hour, I had one of the best treats of my life. An old hotel player like me knows how to play and listen to someone at the same time—it's practically a job requirement—and so

I got to hear Ernie, who remained with his elbow on the Nurses' Station counter the whole time, tell me the entire creation story of "Over the Rainbow" and about the making of *The Wizard of Oz*. Why Yip was called Yip. Anecdotes about Harold Arlen. Apparently he was driving to see a movie with his wife when the melody for "Over the Rainbow" formed in his mind. He was so excited by it that he had to pull the car to the side of the road so he wouldn't get into an accident. Great stories about the Gershwin brothers, and lots of other fantastic music tales from someone who actually knew all the people he was talking about. The time flew by.

Sadly (for me) I had to tell him I needed to leave in a few minutes. He asked if I would play for Deena once more, up close.

As I pulled a chair over to her bedside, she told me there was indeed something special she wanted to hear—another of the great classics, "Summertime," from the show *Porgy and Bess*, music and lyrics by George and Ira Gershwin and Edwin DuBose Heyward.

As I played the last notes of the song, an ascending flourish to the highest register of the guitar, I looked up and saw Deena, eyes closed but not asleep, her face glowing, far, far away from the torments of ICU delirium.

I decided to ask a question. "Deena, I had a strong feeling on Monday and Wednesday that music was very important to you. Are you a musician?" Deena and Ernie smiled at each other, and then she turned to me and murmured, "Yes, I'm a musician." She stopped and glanced back at Ernie. He understood that she wanted him to tell me the rest. She was exhausted still.

"Is she a musician? She can play five instruments!" Ernie said proudly. "She's also a writer and an educator. She was the found-ing chair of the Graduate Musical Theatre Writing Program at the Tisch School of the Arts at New York University and is now the dean emeritus for life of the program. And Deena's written a book that I'm going to send to you because I know you'll love it. It's about the Gershwins, how they worked together as a songwrit-ing team. She practically lived at Ira's house in the last three years of his life. He made his entire collection of their music and memo-rabilia available to her, and gave her endless hours of interviews."

I burst into laughter. They did, too. I'd been playing "Em-braceable You," "The Man I Love," "They Can't Take That Away from Me," and many other Gershwin songs for one of the world's leading authorities on the music of the Gershwins.

The hunch I'd had from the beginning was a good one. I knew many musicians who had the ability to do this, play the room; it's part of connecting to your audience. And I was learning how key an element it is to being able to do thera-peutic music successfully. It felt wonderful that I'd intuited right for Deena, partly because she was so very critically ill, and also because she was a fellow musician and a kindred spirit.

I had to go home then, but Deena, Ernie, and I made plans to stay in touch. This was rare for me as a musician in the SICU. Usually I didn't know the patients' fates once they left the unit and their beds were filled anew. This was uncharted territory, and it was exciting. Though we didn't know it then, we would continue to play important roles in each other's lives.

In the alien world of the SICU, Deena had found something familiar: the music that had meant so much to her throughout her life, both at work and home. A diagnosis of delirium means that the brain is temporarily failing, and for Deena it was definitely hard to make sense of the world around her. The music from the Great American Songbook must have seemed like a beacon of light, something to guide her back to her sense of self. In the confusion of the SICU, those Gershwin tunes stood out as something that made sense. They spoke her language.

I had seen the way music could take away anxiety and stabilize vital signs, the way it could cut through the confusion of brain damage, even add a sense of order to a disorganized mind. But this was different. Here the music had made an impact on an emotional level. The pieces I'd played were all part of Deena's life story, though I hadn't known it at the time. Not consciously, at least. Each song I'd played had plucked at a memory of hers layered deep in her brain. The music had made it past her brain stem and stimulated higher areas of brain function, such as the hippocampus and other areas of the limbic system, those associated with memory and emotion—where those tunes had been recognized and reminded Deena of who she was.

Musical memories are stored as procedural memory, usually associated with routines and repetitive activities. Delirium can affect the parts of the brain responsible for housing episodic memories, the memories that correspond to events in our lives—whereas it leaves the parts of the brain responsible for procedural memory intact. This is why many patients recall very little of their time in the SICU: delirium replaces their memories with a state of confusion.

I can only imagine Deena's relief when she heard familiar music. Her brain must have processed the music and used it as a way to access moments of her life and give her a sense of emotional stability. Luckily for her, the ICU Delirium was temporary and after a few days it was behind her. For people suffering from dementia, and especially Alzheimer's disease, music is a way of tapping into their past. As Oliver Sacks has said, "The past which is not recoverable in any other way is embedded, as if in amber, in the music, and people can regain a sense of identity." Musical memory, buried in the oldest parts of our brain, survives the ravages of the disease and can create a bridge to the past both for the patient and for family and friends. When patients who are "locked in" in so many ways—unable to speak or socialize or interact with their environment—listen to music from their past, an immediate change can be seen. Their faces brighten, their eyes grow alert, they talk and become animated. There is a lingering effect, too, for a while after they stop listening to the music.

In Deena's case of delirium, music became the key to her self. It restored her identity.

Music has been used therapeutically throughout history in a way that was congruent with society's contemporary theories and perceptions about illness.

In preliterate societies, illness was looked at as a punishment, and using music was a way to appease some supernatural power or whoever was doing the punishing so that the illness would be mitigated. So we have that model.

After that we have the model of the "four humors"*—in other words, the balance of the four humors—as the preeminent medical model of perceiving illness that lasted for a couple thousand years . . . and eventually it gets tied to the four parts of four-part harmony in music.

—Bryan Hunter, Ph.D., LCAT, MT-BC,
author interview

*Hippocrates of Kos (460–377 BCE) is universally recognized as the father of modern medicine, which is based on observation of clinical signs and rational conclusions, and does not rely on religious or magical beliefs. Hippocratic medicine was influenced by the Pythagorean theory that nature was made of four elements (air, water, fire, and earth), and the body consisted of four metabolically corresponding fluids or "humors" (blood—air; phlegm—water; yellow bile—fire; black bile—earth). The right balance and purity of the four humors was considered essential to maintaining health.

11

Through the Gate

PAIN IS A CONSTANT in the world of the SICU. I see it in the strained faces of patients and in the infusion pumps that say in bright-red lights FENTANYL or PROPOFOL; I hear it as the nurses make their rounds, asking, "Are you okay? Are you in pain?"

As Dr. Stephan Quentzel, medical director of the Louis Armstrong Center for Music and Medicine, says, "The expectation after surgery is that she'll have pain, that she's in a place that is about pain."

I was talking with him about a patient I'd played for that morning, a frail woman in her sixties who had curled up in the upper-left part of her bed. She was writhing in pain saying, "It hurts, it hurts," over and over, but she was so emotionally distant, so caught up in her own world, that she couldn't communicate anything beyond those words. I'd pulled up a chair and started playing, improvising calming music that turned out to be effective. Within a couple of minutes, she was clearly less agitated. Her repetition of "it hurts, it hurts" stopped, and her shoulders and face relaxed.

I was meeting with Dr. Quentzel at his office downtown on Fifth Avenue to talk about the role that music can play in reducing patient pain in the SICU. I'd been deeply affected by the pain that Deena, the Gershwin expert, had suffered during her hospital stay and thought Quentzel would help clarify my understanding not only of postsurgical pain but also pain in general. He was well qualified to help me: in addition to being medical director, he's triple board-certified in psychiatry, family medicine, and holistic medicine.

"You try to understand the physiology and the psychology and the interpersonal aspects of what she's experiencing when she's writhing in pain. But there's also an expectation that she's supposed to have pain, and I imagine that she's living up to that expectation in part. Every time the nurse comes by and asks her if she's in pain that reinforces it. You know what it's like with a two-year-old child who falls down and only cries if you say, 'Are you okay?' So you never say, 'Are you okay?'—you just scoop them up and continue on the way. This woman is no two-year-old but there's an expectation set *of being in pain* in such a clinical setting. And so she's in all likelihood living up to the expectations."

The expectation of pain reminded me of a book I'd read about the battle of Waterloo. There was a French general who was about to have his leg amputated and he was given just a swig of whiskey. It was 1815 and they didn't have anywhere near the medical capabilities that we have now, so the ability to withstand pain was much greater than it is today. It wasn't just that he was a member of the military with its tradition of stoicism, but that he was also of a different time. The expectations were so different—leg amputation was *supposed* to hurt. When I told Quentzel this story, he agreed.

"And then there are the different meanings of pain. There's the psychology of pain, the interpersonal, the cultural . . ."

I hadn't thought about that before. I'd thought that pain was something physical. Something that we all suffered, and that, although some people had a higher pain tolerance than others, essentially pain was the same for all of us. Clearly, I was wrong.

As Quentzel explained, "The vast majority of the pain experience is only what you can interpret in your brain, so if you're affecting the brain you could be affecting the interpretation of pain and thus the experience of pain. So, medicine affects the interpretation of pain. Music therapies affect the interpretation of pain. But so do all sorts of psychological features, historical, cultural, interpersonal, social. . . . And that speaks to the experience of the amputee in France two hundred years ago as much as it does to the patient you played for this morning."

Pain was much more complex than I had realized. When the woman in Bed 10 was saying, "It hurts, it hurts," she was describing what Quentzel called "a multifactorial experience, the confluence of all sorts of forces meeting in the experience and the expression of pain."

And Deena, too. Her extreme pain was accompanied by the disorienting symptoms of ICU Delirium. Her experience was similar to the patient I'd seen this morning—and yet far removed from it, as well, on a cultural, social, psychological, and biological level. In short, pain is an intensely personal experience. And given that pain does not present in a clear-cut, uniform way across all patients, then what is the best way to treat it?

Quentzel's answer made a great deal of sense to me. He believes that the "multifactorial experience of pain" responds best to an approach that is in itself multifactorial. His response made me think of something I'd read over the years about military history: the classic "best offense" is a double envelopment. In its simplest form, it means that you surround the enemy.

Quentzel laughed. "Yes, that's it. Pain is the enemy as we are describing it. However, it's important to keep in mind that it can be your ally, too, because it alerts you to problems that need to be addressed. But in this case, with Deena and your other patients, you do want a double envelopment, meaning use all the tools at your disposal to treat the symptom, pain, as well as the root causes. That's why music, when applied properly, can be a powerful factor in alleviating pain. Using your military analogy, music is a vital arrow in the quiver. Why? Because among other things, it is universal across cultural, temporal, ethnic, age, and religious specificities."

My time spent in the SICU, the epicenter of critical care, has immersed me in a world of medicine and medical decisions. It was clear to me now that pain—on a physical and psychological level—was central to each patient's SICU experience, and this made me curious to understand more how traditional Western medicine dealt with pain.

I sought out Dr. McMillen for his expertise. A director of a SICU is always aware of, and responsible for, the circumstances of every patient in the unit, especially when there's an extreme situation like ICU Delirium. McMillen had followed Deena's case very closely.

He explained that one reason Deena was in so much pain was that she was in both acute and chronic pain at the same time. The acute pain, which begins suddenly, resulted from the infection in her knee. The chronic pain signals, which can remain active in the nervous system for weeks, months, or years, may have resulted from damage to nerves after her previous surgery. The traditional response to such extreme pain is pain medication. But drug therapies are not always predictable.

"They can have very different patterns of effect and response in patients who are septic, as Deena was," said McMillen. "Sometimes drugs thought not to have any neurologic or cognitive activity at all can have profoundly different and unexpected effects when used in a SICU patient, and the metabolism change can be profound."

McMillen then suggested that I meet with his colleague, Dr. Ronald Kaplan, the attending physician of the Department of Pain and Palliative Care at Beth Israel. I recognized him immediately. I'd seen him in the SICU many times when he was there on consults, and I knew from the nurses and physician's assistants that he was highly regarded.

Almost immediately, he said that pain is always subjective. Just as I'd heard from Quentzel.

"Biologists recognize that the stimuli that cause pain are liable to damage tissue," explained Kaplan. "Accordingly, pain is the experience we associate with actual or potential tissue damage. It is unquestionably a sensation in a part or parts of the body, but it is also always unpleasant and therefore also an emotional experience."

He then remarked that many people report pain even when there isn't any tissue damage, or any likely physiological cause. This usually happens for psychological reasons. But, he continued, "If a patient regards their experience as pain, and if they report it in the same ways as pain caused by tissue damage, it should be accepted as pain."

Which brought me back to the main question of how pain is treated in a hospital setting in the Western tradition. Again, I was thinking of Deena.

"Patients in a medical scenario similar to Deena's are typically provided analgesic, amnesic, and sedative drugs for the time they require this treatment," said Kaplan. "Usually this is provided by continuous intravenous infusions of an opioid, such as Fentanyl or other agents that may possess sedative and/or analgesic properties, such as Propofol."

McMillen had told me that I'd been prescribed Fentanyl during my coma. It is a powerful drug that acts upon specific receptors in the brain to reduce the feeling of pain. I knew that opioids in general could cause euphoria followed rapidly by dysphoria. I'd experienced it myself. I wondered whether this was the cause of Mr. G's slide into dysphoria, too. I also knew that Propofol was a key cause in the death of pop star Michael Jackson—dangerous if used improperly. These medications clearly came with side effects.

I wondered whether treating pain with drugs was only addressing the physical aspect of pain, and not the psychological side. Perhaps the fact that pain is an emotional experience is a crucial entry point in understanding why music can be so effective in pain management. Kaplan agreed.

When I asked him his professional opinion about the use of therapeutic music in conjunction with traditional pain management techniques, he told me he was impressed with what he'd seen when music was effectively applied. He read to me part of a paper by Memorial Sloan Kettering Cancer Center music therapist Lucanne Magill Bailey, published in the *Journal of Pain and Symptom Management*.

"As a complement to the pharmacologic management techniques, my experience is that music therapy in pain and symptom management in the care of critically ill patients can be very effective in helping ameliorate pain and suffering. It can alter affective, cognitive, and sensory processes, may decrease pain perception by distraction, and when the patient is receptive it can change mood, increase control and use of prior skills, and is especially effective in relaxation. Music therapy works in conjunction with traditional medical treatment for pain control. As a treatment modality, music therapy offers great diversity and a range of benefits to patients with pain and suffering."

However, Kaplan had a word of caution, too. "Studies I've read have found that the corollary occurs: used inappropriately, music can aggravate pain sensation."

I agreed completely and said, "I always make sure my guitar's in tune before I start playing for someone on the precipice." We both laughed, even though we both knew I was absolutely serious. Being in tune makes a huge difference in creating the sympathetic vibration that can connect on the deepest levels with a patient, which is so important for the music to be enlivening and not agitating.

Before I played for Deena, I could sum up in one sentence what people told me about how music helped them get through pain; "It takes your mind off it." I'd seen it happen hundreds of times. But now I wondered how. How exactly did music take someone's mind off pain? Was there a specific physiological mechanism that allowed music to have such an ameliorating effect?

In 1965, Dr. Ronald Melzack, a Canadian psychologist, and Dr. Patrick David Wall, a British neuroscientist, introduced their gate control theory of pain. To this day, it is generally accepted that modern pain research began with its publication and it is still the only theory of pain that accurately offers a physiological explanation for the effect of psychology in pain perception. It goes a long way in explaining why music is able to act so effectively as a pain inhibitor.

The genesis of the theory began in the early 1950s at McGill University in Montreal, where Melzack was working on his Ph.D. thesis. He was studying the emotional behavior in dogs and made a discovery: dogs raised with very little sensory input felt pain differently than dogs raised in a normal home setting. The background of the animals had an impact on how they felt pain. This idea differed from all the theories that came before it, which posited a simple cause-and-effect mechanism—that a pain stimulus is transmitted from the peripheral nervous system to the brain.

One of the other things that stoked his thinking was research done during and following World War II by Dr. Henry Beecher, who noted that out of a significant number of soldiers seriously wounded on the Anzio beachhead in Italy in 1944, only one out of five required morphine. When Beecher returned to his medical practice after the war he noticed that patients who had just undergone surgery—and had similarly serious wounds to the soldiers—were more likely to require morphine (one out of three). This led him to think about the importance of the meaning of the injuries to each group of patients. "The soldiers were not unhappy about their wounds," said Beecher. "Suddenly they had a ticket home. But the civilians considered the necessity for surgery a disaster." This indicated that the prevailing concept that the greater the pain stimulus, the greater the intensity of the pain felt in the brain was not always the case. Other factors, including emotional ones, were also involved.

In 1959, Melzack joined the faculty at MIT where he met Patrick Wall, who also felt that psychology and environment were key factors in how people felt pain. As Melzack later said, "In thinking about how that might work I began to think of something that would sort of shut the input going up to the brain, or open it up."

What could do that? A gate, or gates, that could open or close depending on various factors. By 1965, Melzack and Wall had developed their gate control theory of pain and published the article.

According to the theory, pain signals are transmitted from an injury, via the spinal cord, to synapses that receive the pain information in the brain. The synapses act as gates that open and close in response to pain impulses. When the gates are closed, the pain signal is unable to reach the brain. Non-painful input—such as music—closes the gates to painful input.

My neuroscientist friend, Dr. Kamran Fallahpour, gave me a simple analogy one afternoon when we were discussing his own research into pain management. He said, "Imagine people are coming to your home, and to do so they have to pass through a gate and only one person at a time is going through it. That person personifies pain. Many other people just like him follow through the gate, one after another. You're going to have a very unpleasant gathering. But then imagine you have a lot of musicians already in the house and some of them are leaving. On their way out they are taking up a lot of space in the gateway, so fewer pain people can get in, and the musicians remaining upstairs are making a joyous sound. You will feel a lot better that way if this is what is happening!"

So Melzack and Wall's gate control theory allows us to see how once Deena heard music, music that she loved, her sensation of pain diminished, her analgesics were able to be cut back, and she could eventually slide back into a non-delirious state of mind.

I have seen the amazing ways music can help patients navigate their own experiences of pain. I strongly believe that the time I spend with patients is beneficial, but equally important is their regular exposure to music they enjoy. In this way, the tunes can keep playing in their head even after the musician has left the room. Those are the musicians in Fallahpour's analogy who remain in the house. But the patient still needs the regular input of external music to keep the house party going.

There are many research projects studying the effects of music on pain perception. One in particular is especially illuminating.

A participant places his or her hand in a bucket of ice water while listening to a recording of loud and unpleasant industrial sounds. The experimenter records the amount of time the subject can keep their hand in the water before the pain becomes unbearable. Time is then given to dry the hand and allow it to return to its original temperature. Next the subject is asked to pick a favorite piece of music and listen to it while placing his or her hand back in the ice water. The majority of subjects are able to keep their hands in the bucket for almost twice as long with the favorite music. I can think of no other experiment where it is as easy to imagine both the gate control theory of pain and the power music has to affect the comprehensive health of a patient.

It is clear from the ever-increasing understanding by the mainstream practitioners of modern medicine that there is a need for more music as pain medicine, be it music therapy or the use of visiting artists/medical musicians alongside conventional medicine. Deena Rosenberg, the woman I described to Dr. Quentzel, and many more patients who are helped around the world every day this way are the real data that make this a convincing argument.

Music continued to retain its importance as a medical cure for royalty during [the Baroque] period. For example, in 1737, the Queen of Spain engaged the services of the famous Italian singer, Farinelli, to rouse King Philip V from his acute melancholia. Farinelli's efforts had such a beneficial effect that he was subsequently employed as a personal singer to the king and he sang every night to keep King Philip in good spirits.

—**Jacqueline Schmidt Peters,**
Music Therapy: An Introduction

Just Don't Kill the Patient

AN ATTENDING PHYSICIAN was explaining to a nurse how a new medical device worked while awaiting the arrival of a patient from the OR. After giving directions for a minute or so he saw that the nurse, a quick learner, would be able to figure out the rest on his own. He turned to walk away and over his shoulder had one last comment, a Parthian shot, delivered with perfect timing:

"Just don't kill the patient."

(If you lose your sense of humor in a place like this, it's time to leave.)

I now had a new adage to add to "soothing and healing" regarding the use of music in the SICU. Just don't kill the patient.

Joking aside, very important advice, because if music has so much power that it can heal, and even save a life, then certainly it could have the opposite effect.

In August 2011, I was listening to a radio broadcast featuring a doctor who'd been studying the effects of music played during surgery. It was a call-in show and a young physician joined the conversation. He told this story: When he was a medical student he was on a cardiovascular surgery rotation and assisted during an operation. The surgeon was a fan of heavy metal rock music and played it during the surgery. Very loud. The patient wasn't doing well and ended up having ventricular fibrillation, went into cardiac arrest, and died.

I couldn't believe a surgeon would play that kind of music during that kind of an operation. I don't *know* if it was the music that killed the patient, but my hunch is that it's a distinct possibility. At full volume this music could have pushed the patient over the cliff. I was on the edge of the precipice once and the right music pulled me back. I don't doubt for a second, from what I've seen in the past six years, that the opposite could happen. The fact is the patient died, and a very important question is, do you choose the music for the patient's needs, or the doctor's?

So—one of the most important decisions you make as a medical musician is choosing what music you play.

Right from the beginning people would ask me what it's like to be a resident musician in a surgical intensive care unit. By far the question most often asked is, how do you know what to play for patients who are critically ill and not able to say what they'd like to hear? This is the story I always tell to answer that question:

One day shortly after arriving, I was walking past Bed 2 and Christine Wiest, one of the PAs, asked me to play at the patient's bedside. The woman had a gauze bandage wrapped around the top of her head and appeared to be sleeping. I glanced at her chart. She was in her midsixties. Chris explained the patient had undergone successful brain surgery the day before and was now heavily sedated. Their main concern was that her blood pressure was high. It hadn't been below 165 from the time they'd wheeled her in.

Laypeople associate two numbers with blood pressure, as in 120 over 80. The staff in a SICU only refer to the systolic number, the larger number, which measures the pressure in the arteries when the heart beats. The smaller number, the diastolic, measures the pressure between heartbeats when the heart muscle is resting. As in music, it's the beat that counts.

Different drug therapies had been used but nothing had gotten her lower than 165. Normally, if the systolic number is between 140 and 159 it's considered high blood pressure, Stage 1 hypertension. But stress can cause spikes in blood pressure and a SICU is by its nature stressful, so concerns only arise if it's 160 or above and stays that way without medication resolving the issue. As was the case with this patient. Literally from the first day I started, we'd all seen that music had the potential to lower blood pressure. I'd quickly found that playing music with a medium tempo, a beautiful melody, and flowing harmonies—for example, the Gershwins' "Someone to Watch Over Me"—would in most cases cause the patient to relax. You could actually watch the blood pressure numbers drop within a minute or so, sometimes less. I'd done this hundreds of times already and considered it the easiest thing to do of all the different situations I encountered.

If the patient can't tell you what they want, you search for clues. I looked at her name on the chart and asked her nurse if she knew where the woman was from. She told me the patient's niece had visited earlier and mentioned the patient was from Puerto Rico.

When I first moved to New York in 1975, one of my neighbors, José, an actor born and raised in Puerto Rico, had just gotten a grant to do Puerto Rican folklore shows in the city public schools, and he hired me to be his guitarist. There were two beautiful ballads in particular that I'd never forgotten, "Verde Luz" ("Green Light") and "En Mi Viejo San Juan" ("In My Old San Juan"). I always had the sheet music in one of my folders.

I took out the ballads and began to play the entrancing melody of "Verde Luz." For the first couple of minutes I just looked back and forth at the music and the patient. I didn't even bother checking the vital signs monitor. This tune was a well-established go-to piece for lowering blood pressure. Finally, I did look up and saw that her blood pressure had indeed changed.

Unfortunately, in the wrong direction.

It was now 168. I wasn't concerned, though, because I knew that a person might have a bad association with a particular song—maybe there was a romantic breakup or some other negative emotional situation attached to it that brought up stressful memories. I turned to the next song, "En Mi Viejo San Juan."

After only a minute, I looked at the monitor. Her blood pressure was now 170. The next piece in the folder was my old standby, "Someone to Watch Over Me." This time I looked at the monitor in less than thirty seconds. I was stunned. 172. I knew that if it passed 180 she'd be in a hypertensive crisis requiring emergency care. In a critically ill patient that is very serious, and without an intervention, it can be fatal. I remembered an improvisation I'd often used to calm highly agitated patients, a repeating rhythmic pattern that sounded like water flowing in a babbling brook. It had never failed to work. I decided to make one more effort. In the next ten seconds I watched the number climb to 175 and at that moment I was the most scared I've ever been in my life. All that went through my mind was: I'm not helping her, this is very serious, I'd better stop and get assistance.

But as I tensed my leg muscles and began to stand I remembered the nurse who'd long ago told me that what she enjoyed most about being a critical care nurse was the detective work. In that moment I thought of Archie Goodwin of the Nero Wolfe crime novels. Archie was Wolfe's right-hand man. His instructions from Wolfe were that when alone and in a dangerous situation he was to "act in the light of experience as guided by intelligence."

The brain can make connections, especially in a crisis, at the speed of light. As far as I could tell, I was responsible for this crisis. A split second after thinking of Archie's instructions I had a hunch based on experience. I sat down. I would play my hunch but only watch the monitor, not the patient. If it clicked up just one number I'd stop immediately and get Chris or a nurse or doctor as fast as possible. I looked over my shoulder; several staff members were just a few yards away, at another patient's bed.

The music for the hunch was right on the stand. I started. For about thirty seconds nothing moved. A minute went by. Nothing. Still 175. Then I saw the LED light flicker. The number changed. 174.

About five minutes after I began, Chris and the nurse returned. By then, it was already under 160. I heard Chris say, "Cool," and leave again. The nurse stayed. I kept going even once the patient had leveled off at 135, playing until I felt it was safe to stop. The first thing I asked the nurse was if they had changed anything while I was playing—medication, anything. She said no. Understanding the reason for my question she said the change in blood pressure was almost certainly caused by the music. Chris came back and checked a few things—the ventilator, the infusion pump, some of the lines—and I asked her the same question. No, she hadn't changed anything. She looked once more at the monitor, I got a smile and a pat on the back, and she left again. I let out what was probably my all-time personal record for a long sigh of relief.

What was the hunch that I played that had worked so well? Bach. Of course. But not just any Bach. *Fast* Bach.

In that moment, when I'd thought of the nurse's detective remark, I'd remembered two things.

First, I already knew the effectiveness of Bach's music in post-brain-surgery cases. I had played for dozens of post-brain-surgery patients with complications of some sort, a common occurrence with that kind of surgery but almost always short-lasting. Second, in the year I'd done the Puerto Rican folklore shows with José, I'd played a lot of salsa and merengue music, music with a quick tempo and strong and steady beat, and the audiences loved it. So I combined the two, and it worked.

The lingering effect of music, what Dr. McMillen has described as the blossoming effect, was the case with the patient in Bed 2. Her blood pressure remained stable for the remaining two days she was in the SICU, a factor in her short stay.

So, the answer to that most often asked question is: you never know. There is no default position. You start out with what you think will be soothing and healing and you go from there, relying on your experience and following any clues you can detect. You act in the light of experience as guided by intelligence. As research psychologist Gary Klein puts it, "Intuition is really a matter of learning how to see—of looking for cues or patterns that ultimately show you what to do."

Luckily, this story is a one and only for me. I have never had such a potentially catastrophic experience before or since. If I had, I would have been long gone from the SICU. For two reasons.

First, the staff, especially the attending physicians, are extremely protective of their patients. If you are not helping, you are gone. Second, my nerves couldn't take much more of the roller-coaster ride I was on that day. I would have left on my own.

The next most often asked question has been: What is the most effective music to play for a patient? That's an easy answer. If the patient is awake and lucid, the patient's favorite music is *always* best. That's why it's so important to have a wide-ranging music repertoire. We have people in the SICU from all over the world. It's interesting that in most music and medicine research studies, the best results are seen when participants self-select the music.

But the problem remains—80 percent or more of the time the patient can't tell you what they want because they're not able to. Not just in cases of heavy sedation, coma, or vegetative states. Given the stressful environment, powerful pain medications, lack of sleep, and general disorientation, the question, "What music would you like to hear?" is simply too hard for most patients to handle.

During my first six months of playing in the SICU, I kept a journal and wrote down everything I played each day. Because I couldn't play from memory, and had a large collection of sheet music, I had the advantage of trying all kinds of music. I found a great deal of music was effective. There were Mozart adagios that I arranged—slow, beautiful pieces, often cited in studies of healing music—as well as some of the smaller movements from Beethoven's piano sonatas. Especially good was the sprightly Allegretto from the famous Moonlight Sonata.

Inspired by the diverse patient population and staff at Beth Israel, I arranged music from many different cultures. A great find, suggested by Dr. Fallahpour, was the music of Ostad Elahi, who played the Persian *tanbūr,* an ancient, long-necked lute. I took melodies from China, India, Scotland, Peru. Everywhere.

As the months and then years passed, I saw that certain music had a high rate of effectiveness. There were three bodies of work in particular: Bach, Gershwin, and the Beatles. There were also two individual pieces I noticed that were exceptionally effective. One was Franz Schubert's "Ständchen," a serenade, written in the 1820s in Vienna. The other was "Bohemian Rhapsody," written by Freddie Mercury in 1975 in London.

Time and again, I'd seen Bach effect incredible change in a patient's well-being—and medical outcome. From my own experience, to that of the "Russian patient" with the misfiring synapses, to the patient with the racing blood pressure, Bach's music has consistently soothed and healed. I decided to contact Arthur W. Harvey, who had inspired me so greatly when he said, "Of all the music we tested in medical school with patients, colleagues, and others, Bach's music consistently made the brain work in a balanced way better than any other genre." I wanted to find out why this was so.

It turns out that Bach's music has been a cornerstone of Arthur Harvey's long life in music and healing.

"As a church organist I have included at least one selection of J. S. Bach for almost every service I've ever played," he told me. "For personal listening, Bach's music has always been at the top of my preference list. As an educator, there have been several primary questions that motivated me to explore the power of the music of Bach. The first one is, *why* is Bach's music so relevant, adaptable, and universally appreciated?"

When Dr. Harvey, DMA (Doctor of Musical Arts), was on the faculty of the School of Medicine at the University of Louisville in Kentucky in the late '80s, he created a course, Music in Medicine, which enabled medical students to pursue research in a variety of areas, including the study of different genres of music.

"We focused on seven: Chant, Baroque, Classical, Gospel, New Age, Jazz, and Folk. The conclusion at the end of two years of study, including the use of brain scans, was that the music of the Baroque era was the most healthful, because it stabilized the different rhythms of the body and mind—mental, physical, and emotional—which allowed for greater concentration and focus. Bach's music consistently showed the best results in this regard."

They followed many avenues of exploration, among them: the

source of Bach's inspiration for composing, the historical period in which he wrote, and for whom he composed his enormous repertoire.

Why does Bach's music balance the brain so well? My thought was that the perfect counterpoint in his music (voices that are interdependent harmonically yet independent in rhythm) balances the brain as there is always more than one important focus of attention, and his inventiveness in every phrase means that you're never certain how something will resolve until it does—but when the resolution occurs it's always completely satisfying.

"You're on the right track," Arthur replied, "but it goes far beyond that. Using a current neuromusicological model, Bach's music utilizes both chordal music (music characterized by harmony) and contrapuntal textures (the interweaving melodies) somewhat equally, which provides for music processing in both left and right hemispheres of the human brain. A descriptive characteristic of his music and music of his time is the significance of balance.

"You hear sounds that are soft and loud, high and low, short and long. Rhythms that are slow and fast, simple and complex. Melodies and harmonies that have enormous stylistic variety. Also very important—a mixture of these different types of sound, for example, as happens in the Bach piece most people know by name or simply recognize by the melody, Jesu, Joy of Man's Desiring."

"Jesu. Yes, it's one of the most soothing pieces I play in the SICU, for the patients *and* the staff," I said.

"I'm not surprised," Harvey continued. "In larger works, like the *St. Matthew Passion*, the use of all the music techniques at his disposal in one piece of music creates a level of stimulation throughout so much of the brain that would go a long way in explaining the seemingly miraculous effect that music had in your coma."

In my case, Bach's music of balance clearly had all the right ingredients to stimulate the brain stem and then reach the higher areas of brain function.

"If it's all in perfect balance," I said, "does that mean the listener's brain is receiving a great deal of stimulation but the circuits are not being overloaded, and that would explain why, over and over, I have seen such dramatic results with patients, particularly when they are sedated or in vegetative or coma states?"

"Yes, exactly right."

We talked for a while longer about music and medicine in general. Just a couple of Bach guys hanging out.

The effectiveness of the music of the Gershwins and the Beatles in helping patients did not surprise me. These were tunes that evoked musical memories—often of a patient's youth, of singing, dancing, happy times. As, for example, when the Beatles' "Here Comes the Sun" or the Gershwins' "Embraceable You" is processed by the auditory cortex, a patient's emotional connection to the music will light up the main parts of the brain stimulated by musical memories: the amygdala, the nucleus accumbens, and the hippocampus. The nucleus accumbens is activated by peak emotional experiences but it is also triggered as soon as music is experienced as pleasurable.

Of course another factor is simply that these bodies of work are not only brilliant, they are extraordinarily well known and loved all over the world. As Mozart once wrote about his own music in a letter to his father, "There are passages . . . from which the connoisseurs alone can derive satisfaction; but these passages are written in such a way that the less learned cannot fail to be pleased, though without knowing why."

I noticed from the beginning that Franz Schubert's Ständchen also cut across all cultural lines. It seems to reach more people on a deeply emotional level than any other single piece. Schubert was composing in Vienna, a crossroads between East and West, and I believe that is reflected in the poignant melody. But it goes beyond that. The yearning quality has a touch of the blues in it, too, and you can also hear the harmonies of modern popular music. These are not just my observations. People from many diverse backgrounds have told me what they hear in this music and why it moves them so much. In almost every case it makes a strong emotional connection.

When I was a young guitarist I played five nights a week in a small restaurant—The Cellar in the Sky at Windows on the World. The first night I played Ständchen I repeated it several times. Throughout the evening the maître d', two waiters, and a busboy all told me it reminded them of where they grew up. They were from Portugal, the United States, Thailand, and Jordan.

Ständchen is a great example of music as "the universal language of mankind"—as poet Henry Wadsworth Longfellow wrote. Its universality is key when playing for critically ill people from all over the world.

Over the years I've received many emails from patients and their friends and family. One of my favorites was from a patient by the name of Gordon Taylor, a young man who fell down a flight of stairs while visiting New York from his home in Seattle. He had suffered massive head injuries, and was given a 40 percent chance of survival when the ambulance arrived at the hospital. I played for him just once. I remember his entire head was covered in white gauze bandages with holes cut for his eyes and mouth so he could be intubated and breath via a ventilator.

"I don't remember much from those first few days in the hospital, but I do remember the guitar. The music soothed me, and I was grateful for something to focus on besides my pain and fear. Specifically, I remember giving you a thumbs-up as you played 'Bohemian Rhapsody.' Listening to you play guitar was one of the few moments of peace that I can remember from the entirety of my stay at Beth Israel. . . . I am also a musician and as I play these days I often pause to reflect on the healing power of music. . . . I thank you."

"Bohemian Rhapsody" draws upon not only different kinds of music—ballad, opera, rock—but the composer himself. Freddie Mercury was born in Zanzibar to Parsi parents from the Indian state of Gujarat and moved to England when he was a teenager. While I've not yet found a study that tracks how specific types of world music impact healing, I like to think that this combination of musical and cultural traditions must surely contribute to the song's appeal—and power—as effective musical medicine.

One afternoon when I was having coffee with Deena Rosenberg and Ernie Harburg, long after Deena's ICU Delirium, I was telling them about the music that I found to be most effective. They gave me an insight into the common bond of this repertoire, the unifying link, and I finally understood how it all connected. It was right there in front of me all that time but I couldn't see the forest for the trees.

Ernie's grin was ear to ear. "Andrew, with the exception of the Bach they're all instrumental arrangements you've done of vocal music! And even with the Bach, what saved you in your coma was a huge vocal piece, and you've told me that a lot of the Bach you play is arrangements you've done of chorale music, like Jesu, Joy of Man's Desiring, which is vocal music."

Deena, whose knowledge of the song repertoire is encyclopedic, expanded further. "And in each case, especially if we include the St. Matthew Passion, there is the synergy of more than one person creating the music. Bach's music was set to a libretto by Picander. Gershwin music is George the composer and Ira the lyricist. The Beatles' music resulted from a collaboration of the four of them with their record producer, George Martin. Schubert's Ständchen is set to a poem by Ludwig Rellstab. And although Freddie Mercury wrote 'Bohemian Rhapsody' it was shaped into final form by input from all the players in Queen during the recording sessions."

"When you have these collaborations," Ernie added, "the creativity sparks all over the place. Yes, it's very powerful music when the starting point of the talent is so high. But the most important point is this: the music is connected to words, and they all tell a story. I have no doubt that when you play your instrumental arrangements of vocal music for patients, and the music goes into their ears, it is going in very deep because it's not just the memories of melodies; for many patients you are also activating the parts of the brain that store the words, as well, so there is greater processing and you see greater results. Of course, you've also had these extraordinary results with Bach's purely instrumental music, but let's face it"—and he grinned again—"Bach is Bach!"

Although Ernie isn't a brain expert, it turns out that scientific research backs up his gut reaction: the brain is stimulated both by music and language components of songs with lyrics. The question has long been, does the brain process the words and lyrics separately or as one? Daniela Sammler of the Max Planck Institute for Human Cognitive and Brain Sciences in Leipzig, Germany, and her research team studied brain activity during fMRI brain scans of people listening to songs. They found that one specific brain region—the superior temporal sulcus (STS)—responded to the songs. The lyrics and tune were processed as one in the middle of the STS, while in the anterior STS only the lyrics seemed to undergo processing. Sammler concluded that after the initial processing of the song as a whole, a more complex evaluation kicks in as the brain figures out the meaning of the words. And then there's the emotional element of songs, too—which would lead to more brain activity.

I thought again of the tremendous work that Deena's brain did that day in extrapolating meaning from the Gershwins' melodies I played to her. 'S wonderful indeed.

In early 2014, a close friend, the eminent historian Albert Fried, invited me to go to a lecture with him on mental illness and creativity presented by Dr. Richard Kogan.

Kogan is a clinical professor of psychiatry at Weill Cornell Medical Center and artistic director of the Weill Cornell Music and Medicine Program. He's also a concert pianist, attended the Juilliard School of Music, and later attended Harvard University—where he formed a trio with his Juilliard friend and Harvard roommate, Yo-Yo Ma.

The lecture-concert featured the music and psychological state of famous Russian composer and pianist Sergei Rachmaninoff, and it gave me a new way to think about the music I played in the SICU. I contacted Kogan and he graciously offered to meet with me.

We spoke at length and he shared his insights.

"A disproportionate number of the greatest composers have suffered from signs and symptoms of psychiatric disorders. Tchaikovsky was suicidally depressed, Beethoven had persecutory delusions, Schumann lived the final years of his life in an insane asylum, Mahler sought treatment from Freud, and Rachmaninoff's beloved Second Piano Concerto was dedicated to the psychiatrist who cured him of his crippling depression and writer's block."

Kogan continued, "While it's important not to overromanticize mental illness—most depressed individuals are too paralyzed to write a symphony and most psychotic individuals are too disorganized to produce a work of art that is coherent—the suffering associated with mental illness can lead to bursts of creative inspiration that are less likely to come from an individual that is emotionally content. For many of the greatest composers music has been profoundly therapeutic."

In other words, artists who used their music to alleviate their own suffering composed some of the greatest music ever written, which in turn has the effect of ameliorating the suffering of others.

I asked Kogan about George Gershwin, a particular hero of mine, whose music had helped me innumerable times.

"George Gershwin had a host of behavioral problems as a youngster. He regularly engaged in fistfights, stole food from pushcarts, and even set fires. All of this changed when he heard a classmate play the violin at a school assembly—Maxie Rosenzweig, who became the noted concert violinist Max Rosen. He was so entranced by the sounds that he vowed he would devote the rest of his life to his music education. He persuaded his parents to let him take piano lessons and he began to immerse himself in music. Gershwin summed up his childhood this way: 'I spent my young years making a nuisance of myself. Studying the piano turned a bad boy into a good boy.' George's story is one of the best illustrations of the capability of music to transform the lives of youngsters."

Bach was known for his strong and stable character, but he lived with his own fair share of tragedy. His mother died when he was nine and his father died eight months later. His beloved first wife, Maria Barbara, died when he was thirty-five, and only ten of his twenty children survived to adulthood. Bach was no stranger to emotional suffering.

Schubert wrote "Ständchen" while desperately ill just before he died. Freddie Mercury's "Bohemian Rhapsody" likely came out of a very personal place and was probably written as he was struggling with his sexuality. Of the four Beatles, John Lennon suffered in his personal life the most, but they composed nearly all their best known music, including "Here Comes the Sun," "In My Life," "Yesterday," "If I Fell," "Strawberry Fields Forever," "She's Leaving Home"—the tunes that I've observed have the greatest effect—under the enormous stress imposed by their stardom and the growing discord in the group that ended the Beatles as a band of brothers.

When I play music as a medical musician, my intent is to find a way for the music to connect with the patient on an emotional level. My thoughts often come back to the *St. Matthew Passion* and the way it resonated so deeply within me. I've wondered whether it might have been the only piece that could have saved me at that crucial moment.

Recently, I heard the *Requiem* by French composer Thierry Lancino and felt a similar vibration, a shiver down the spine. Perhaps this music would have saved me, too. It made me think about the composer's intent when he or she writes music.

I couldn't ask Bach about his music. However, I *could* ask Thierry. He's been my next-door neighbor for almost twenty years. I told him how much the *Requiem* had affected me, and wondered why that was so.

"I had a revelation when I was a child," started Lancino. "When I was eight years old I got a record from my grandfather. Until then I had no particular connection with music. It was a small record, the kind they did back then. On one side was the slow movement, the Largo, from Bach's *Concerto for Two Violins in D Minor.* I listened to that and something happened to me, something very exciting. I'd never heard any classical music before. It spoke to me. I remember jumping around and being so excited and going to my mother and saying, 'I understand something. I understand music is something else. It's something we don't know!'

"I think looking back, at the past, my state of mind when I compose is to convince people of this revelation I had as a little boy. I am always trying to reach people specifically on an emotional level, as I was reached when I first heard that Bach recording.

"In the performances of the *Requiem* I see people crying. I've had hundreds of letters from people telling me how much it moved them. One woman told me, 'I had not cried for thirty years. Now you've opened a place for me to go, I can cry again.'

"If I had lived only for this, it would be enough for me. So, I feel very completed with this *Requiem*."

Lancino stopped for a moment, and then laughed. "Although I want to do more, of course, but I have finally transmitted in this piece the faith, the revelation I had when I first heard the Bach when I was a little boy."

The next day he sent me this quote from the concert program, a translation from the French:

"I have wished that this *Requiem,* in an intimate manner, penetrates the imagination of everyone, impregnates, and reaches the remote region where souls take shelter. So that, in a glimpse, they may touch the mystery of death, even by the tip of a finger."

I'll never know, but I like to think Bach might have said something very similar about his *St. Matthew Passion*.

What do we know about Bach's intentions with his music? Very little. He wrote his music, but he wrote very little about why he did so. But we do have this from his pen:

"The aim and final reason of all music should be none else but the Glory of God and the recreation of the mind and spirit."

Although choice of music is clearly paramount in the role of a medical musician, I believe the instrument you play counts for a lot. A classical guitar is an ideal, maybe *the* ideal instrument for critical care music. It is portable, and can play complete music, meaning you can play the melody, harmony, and bass line simultaneously, which means that one person, taking up very little space, can have the effect of an ensemble. The classical guitar, with its nylon (or gut) strings, also has an inherently warm, intimate sound.

An old friend of mine, Ben Verdery, chairman of the guitar program at Yale School of Music, explained, "The thing about the guitar that's so extraordinary is that it's an international voice—you can play a folk song from any country and it can sound like a *pipa*, a *koto*, or a *cuatro*—more than any other instrument, it's like a chameleon, it can mimic the sound of so many different plucked string instruments, the type of stringed instruments most common since antiquity. It's a vital connection to the extremely diverse patient population you play for that makes the guitar so unique. The patients hear not only a favor-

ite tune but also a favorite *sound*. That makes such a big difference. And you can take it anywhere without amplification and
the volume is great because you can play soft but you can kick it
up. And the patient sees you right there—passion is natural to
the guitar and the patient sees that and thinks, 'I want to get
out of the hospital and get back to my gardening, or writing, or
cooking,' or whatever they do."

I've been an endorsee of D'Addario Strings since 1982, and I
drove out to the factory on Long Island to meet with CEO Jim
D'Addario and the director of research and development, Fan-
Chia Tao.

Fan had this to say about the guitar: "Although instruments
like the violin and cello are frequently mentioned as sounding
most like a human voice, a great case can be made for the guitar. The frequency range of a classical guitar matches that of
human voices more closely than any other instrument, from the
lowest male to the highest female. The loudness of a guitar is
similar to that of a normal human voice speaking and singing in
everyday situations. Therefore, a guitar is ideally suited for playing in a small room. Unlike many other instruments, the guitar
cannot sustain a continuous note. Once a string is plucked, the
sound starts to decay. A skilled performer, however, can give the
illusion of playing legato, smoothly, filling in the silences between
notes. This is similar to human speech, and how a mother might
sing to her baby."

Classical guitarist Andrés Segovia understood the guitar like
few others in history. A few months before he died in 1987 at the
age of ninety-four, he was interviewed by Howard Reich, the music
critic of the *Chicago Tribune*.

"It is the poetry of the guitar that makes people listen," he said. "The most simple tunes, the most gentle ideas, become poetical when played on the guitar."

And these poetics can reach across the noise of the SICU—in the form of Bach, Gershwin, the Beatles, and many others—and deep into a critically ill patient's brain where soothing and healing can begin.

Louis Roger, an eighteenth-century French physician, wrote a serious treatise based on carefully observed case histories and advocated music as therapy to give order to minds craving structure and to stimulate the nervous system through sympathetic vibration, helping them to "throw off the thickened and foreign humors."

—Jacqueline Schmidt Peters,
Music Therapy: An Introduction

13

The Music of Poetry, the Poetry of Music

HURRICANE SANDY HIT New York City on Monday, October 29, 2012. I couldn't get to the SICU that day or on the following Wednesday—mass transit was shut down. By Friday, there was a patchwork way to get through: a subway ride to Times Square and, from there, a shuttle bus ride downtown to Beth Israel. All electricity was still off below Forty-second Street, and as I stared out of the bus windows it looked like a scene in a disaster movie. The stores were all closed and none of the traffic lights worked—not that it mattered. There were few vehicles or residents in sight. Of the civilian kind, that is. Streets bustled with soldiers in uniform—U.S. Army and National Guard—as well as members of the New York Police Department and Fire Department. Their trucks were everywhere, loaded with supplies, especially enormous pallets crammed with plastic gallon containers of drinking water.

Seeing the aftermath of Sandy made me think of another catastrophe. 9/11. I had played for more than twenty years at Windows on the World, the restaurant on the 107th floor of the North Tower of the World Trade Center. Five nights a week for two years, then, after that, at hundreds of private parties in the banquet rooms. Two days before hijackers crashed jets into the Twin Towers, the music agent at Windows called to book me for a corporate breakfast scheduled for the morning of the eleventh. The next day he called again. The host had changed his mind and decided not to have live music. There were over one hundred people at that breakfast, and over eighty staff members on site. Many of them were good friends. Every one of them died that morning, and painful memories returned as I stared out the bus window. On 9/11, I was powerless to be of help to my friends. However, I could be of some use today. A lot of people would undoubtedly be highly stressed-out—patients *and* staff.

Music played a huge role in New York's emotional healing after September 11. The first organized public event after the attacks was a musical one. The New York Philharmonic was to host a gala on September 20 to open music director Kurt Masur's final season. Instead, they changed the program and turned the evening into one of hope and healing beginning with the national anthem—sung by all in attendance—and ending with *A German Requiem* by Johannes Brahms. The orchestra played under the forty-eight-star flag that had been used for concerts during World War II. Apparently, Masur asked the audience not to applaud at the end of the performance, and so they remained silent and respectful, before filing out into the night. It was the first of many such tributes, the community finding solace, strength, and solidarity through music. The psychological and physiological effects would have been manyfold. It is no wonder to me why humans continue to turn to music in difficult times.

I got off the bus at Seventeenth Street, a block from the hospital, and immediately heard a loud rumbling noise. I soon saw the culprits—several huge gas-powered generators. I knew from news reports that the staff of Beth Israel was performing heroic work that week. Several nearby hospitals had been forced to close when their power failed, and many of their patients were sent to Beth Israel, stretching its resources to the breaking point.

Inside the Silver Building, where the SICU was located, all the lights were dim and the air was dank and heavy. Only one elevator was operating in that wing instead of the usual four. On the ride up, an administrator told me that every electronic device that wasn't absolutely necessary was turned off to save power. Most of the computers were down. When I entered the SICU and took my first breath, it was obvious the air quality here was even worse. The fragrant clean smell had disappeared.

The first two staff members I encountered were a physician's assistant named Katrina and a nurse practitioner named Sandy. Our names recalled three of the most devastating hurricanes in American history. As I approached, I said, "Hello, Katrina and Sandy, my name is Andrew." It had the intended effect. They all laughed. They and everyone nearby had a moment's respite. The unit was full, patients in all twelve beds. I'd already decided I'd play longer than usual, for as long as I was needed.

Many doctors, nurses, and staff had been sleeping at the

hospital all week, or had found incredible ways to get there. Dr. Loewy and her music therapy staff were everywhere, helping to calm frayed nerves.

I'd always thought of the SICU as its own little bubble, a microcosm, and it seemed especially true today with the storm raging farther up the East Coast. The elements were out of order. Maybe music would help to balance them.

An elderly patient in Bed 12 had asked if I could go to him right away, so I headed over to his bedside. He was sitting up in one of the special upholstered hospital chairs positioned by each bed for the patients to use. Handsome and slim, he reminded me of the 1930s movie star William Powell. He was evidently tired and his complexion was pallid, but even so he gestured for me to sit in the chair near him. I'd learned that a combination of music and conversation, if the patient wanted to talk, could be a most effective therapy.

Within the first few minutes, I found him to be witty and charming. He told me his name was John Peters. When I asked what he'd like to hear, he leaned forward a little and with a slight tilt of his head said, "Do you know any Bach? I have a friend that often plays Bach on the guitar for me, and I love it."

I smiled. "That's a two thumbs-up request. How about a whole suite?"

"Perfect." He settled back in the chair and closed his eyes.

I've always considered Bach's *First Cello Suite*, so perfectly suited to the guitar, to be ideal musical medicine. Every movement is sheer perfection. It's all lyrical magic, uplifting, each movement a different tempo, rhythm, and mood. It manages to take patients on a journey through the countryside on a gorgeous spring day, away from the SICU and, today, far from the storm's devastation. When I finished the concluding Gigue, a rollicking dance, a real foot tapper that ends with a grand and immensely satisfying final flourish, John opened his eyes. The corners of his mouth curled up. There was a little more color in his face, and he applauded as best he could.

"More music?" I asked.

Leaning forward again and with the same slight tilt of his head, he asked, "By any chance do you know any . . . Jobim?"

"Two in a row, my friend!" I love the music of Antônio Carlos Jobim, one of the originators of Brazilian bossa nova music and one of the most important songwriters of the twentieth century. I'd brought my bossa nova folder that day and picked out five of his best-known tunes: "Meditation," "Wave," "Desafinado," "Girl from Ipanema," and "One Note Samba." I started the intro to "Meditation." John's eyes shut again, but he swayed to the beat the whole time. Bossa nova music does that—at its core is a rhythm based on samba, rhythmic patterns originating from African dance music, giving it a swaying feel rather than the swinging feel of jazz. As soon as I saw him moving to the beat, I felt great. Dance/movement therapy (DMT) and music therapy are obviously joined at the hip, and a fringe benefit of therapeutic music is getting the patient to move, joyfully, in rhythm.

As I played the final chord of "One Note Samba," sharply percussive, sounding like the final hit of a conga drum, he opened his eyes and said, "You know, I was a friend of Tom Jobim. He would sometimes stay with me when he was in New York."

That elicited a classic "eyes popped open and jaw dropped" response. "No kidding! Tell me about it."

Some great stories, all of them affirming something that I'd always heard, that Tom Jobim was an exceptional human being. One was quite funny, describing how Jobim told him a series of bawdy Brazilian jokes as he ironed his pants in the living room. When he died in 1994, a day of national mourning was declared in Brazil.

By this time, John and I had clearly established an excellent rapport. It's always a judgment call if you're going to ask a patient about their illness and surgery. If you think they're open to it, and you guess wrong, the patient can shut down and the bridge you've created between you comes tumbling down. But John had such an open and engaging personality that I took the leap of faith.

"Heart surgery," he said. "Two days ago. I fainted at home but a friend was with me. He called 911—they arrived within minutes and got me to the hospital fast. I was very lucky. Within an hour of my arrival, I had a major heart attack. But then there were some serious complications." He stopped speaking and closed his eyes.

He didn't want to go any further so I said a few encouraging words about how good the medical team was here and moved to my next question. "What do you, or did you, do for a living?"

"A lot of things. I was a longshoreman, worked in construction, the hotel business. I've lived in Westbeth, one of New York's oldest artist communities, for years. I got in there because I'm a poet, always have been, even when I worked those day jobs." He smiled. "My poetry came out of an early love—a passion for storytelling, both in the giving and receiving. It brings me joy. 'Joy' is my favorite word."

"Joy, yes!" I paused, thinking. "John, I've just played for you—if you're feeling up to it, would you recite some of your poetry for me?"

His eyes had a new light in them. He shifted in the chair, sitting taller, then glanced down for a moment, probably deciding what he'd start with. He looked up again but not at me, and began. Softly at first, then gradually the range of his voice broadened.

The first thing I noticed was how musical he was. As he started to recite a poem, his right hand began to move, like a conductor keeping a beat. As soon as he finished the first, he went straight into the next. The poems were short, but as he kept going they grew longer. I still remember certain lines.

"The heart still warm / the spirit strong / Enjoy, enjoy the sparrow's song." When he spoke that one I wondered if the Bach cello suite had transported him to the countryside and lit up the memory center in his hippocampus where the poem was stored.

His hand never stopped keeping the rhythm, but even there it was a subtle dance, and not always predictable in the phrasing. For the first time in the SICU, a patient was performing for me. It was delightful! I sat back and rested my guitar upright on my leg. I felt the oppressive weight of the storm lighten a little.

After a while, John paused. "That's enough poetry for now," he said. "But would you play some more music for me? Do you know any Villa-Lobos? Prelude no. 3? Tom Jobim used to play it for me. He was a pianist, you know, but also played the guitar and that was his favorite piece."

Heitor Villa-Lobos, also Brazilian, was one of the best-known and prolific classical composers of the twentieth century—by the time of his death he'd written over two thousand works. Many consider the music he wrote for the guitar among the finest in the modern repertoire. And, like Jobim, when he died a day of national mourning was declared for him.

"Yes, I know it. I'll play it for you, but first, you say you like stories. I've got one for you. It involves that prelude, and someone I'm sure you've heard of. The Spanish guitarist Andrés Segovia. Did you ever hear him in concert?"

He smiled in recognition. "Oh, *certamente!*"

"Thirty years ago, I had the best music lesson of my life— with Segovia. At the time, he was eighty-six and I was twenty-seven. I never understood the most important part of the lesson until just now, while listening to you.

"I played Prelude no. 3 for him—which is in two sections. The first part went well, and then I started the second section, which is marked *Molto adagio e dolorido*, which basically means 'very slow and sorrowful.'

"I began playing it with a lot of intensity, a lot of vibrato for dramatic effect, and I thought I was nailing it. Then I heard a strange sound, mechanical, like a truck breaking down. But I was on the nineteenth floor of a hotel, and so I played right through it.

"A few more seconds went by and the sound started up again. Like a bad compressor in a refrigerator—but I just kept playing. Finally, I looked up. Just three feet in front of me was the most famous classical guitarist of all time, his eyes popping open wide, staring at me, and hooting.

" 'Whoooooo . . . whoooooo . . . whoooooo . . .' Each hoot

started in a high falsetto and very slowly swooped down really low. I stopped playing and shrugged my shoulders, smiling. 'Okay, what am I doing?'

"Segovia turned very serious. 'What do you say to your wife?' he said in a low voice. 'Do you say, I LOFFF YOOOU!!!?' He was almost shouting. Then, dropping his voice to a whisper, he said, 'Or do you say . . . I love you'?

"These last three words came at me as the essence of what *dolorido* meant, as the sound of deep sorrow and sadness, as if he was saying it to his wife as she lay dying. That was how I needed to play to bring out the meaning of the music. I started the section again. There were no interruptions this time. As the last chord faded away, I looked up, our eyes held, he nodded, and said, 'Good. Next.'

"I'd always thought the fact that he liked my guitar playing and had encouraged me to continue with it was what mattered most. But there was something more important. He taught me how to find the poetry in music."

John sat forward, eyes shining. "Andrew, that's it. Wordsworth once said 'poetry is the spontaneous overflow of powerful feelings: it takes its origin from emotion recollected in tranquility.' And that's what you just did for me with music."

I nodded. He looked brighter, his cheeks pink. I could almost see his brain buzzing with the words of the poems, the memories of his friend Tom Jobim.

I played Prelude no. 3, remembering my few hours with Segovia and especially his lesson. Though neither he nor I knew it at the time, he was teaching me a fundamental part of musical healing. The constant need to be aware of the patient and to step back as a performer to allow room for response to the music on an emotional or cognitive level in a direct or indirect way. I had gilded the lily in my performance for Segovia, instead of letting the poetry of the music itself come through. Now I watched as the music reached John Peters in his chair. His eyes were closed but he was smiling, his hand marking time.

A nurse quietly approached and said, "The patient in Bed 1 asked if you would come over and play for her." I'd been with John for almost an hour. I did need to move on.

As I started to get up, he said, "It was perfect that you were here today."

"Perfect? How so?"

"Because I'm probably going to die tonight. I feel one foot in this world and one foot in the next, and if this is my last day on earth, it was perfect that I got to hear this music I love so much."

I was stunned. For a moment I simply had no idea how to respond. Then I realized there was only one thing I could say.

"I'm so glad I could be here for you today, my friend." We nodded goodbye. I left for Bed 1.

I stayed in the SICU for the rest of the afternoon. On my way out, I passed Bed 12 and stopped for a minute. John was back in bed, in a deep sleep. It was hard to tell if he was breathing.

I walked out into the darkness of the blacked-out city and headed toward the uptown bus. Just as I arrived at Sixth Avenue and Fourteenth Street, the lights—streetlights, building lights, it seemed like every possible light—turned on all at once. It was an almost biblical moment. The power below Forty-second Street had come back on. The crowds of people all around me went silent for seconds, and then in near unison, an enormous long-lasting cheer went up. A sound of joy.

Over the past three years, I'd left on a number of Fridays not knowing if the person I'd just played for, talked to, even befriended would be alive when I returned the following Monday. That has been the most difficult thing to learn to cope with. I was anxious all weekend thinking about John Peters.

On Monday, as I entered the SICU, my heart was beating fast. You make that left turn past Bed 11 and a few steps later you are in front of Bed 12. As I approached, I could see the curtain was open. I knew I would see an empty bed, or another patient, or maybe, just maybe, John Peters. Those few steps were agonizing. And then I was there. I stopped, turned, and looked.

What I saw was the poet, sitting upright in that same chair he'd been in on Friday, with a nurse at his side gently brushing his teeth. John saw me and in an instant there was a twinkle in his eyes and what looked like a sly grin. He lifted his left hand and with index and middle fingers together he did a little "How d'ya do" wave William Powell might have done as Nick Charles in the 1934 comedy *The Thin Man*. I smiled back but kept walking. At first I felt sheer joy—he was alive. Happy as I was, though, I couldn't help but wonder: Had John the Poet taken a little "poetic license" with me in saying he was about to die? If so, bravo, John, ya got me! Just at that moment I almost walked into Dr. Eiref. We'd had a special bond ever since he gave Wendy permission to use my iPod during my coma.

"Dr. Eiref, I played quite a bit for the patient in Bed 12 on Friday, and he told me that he thought he was probably going to die that night. Was that real?"

"Actually, yes. Things looked very serious that afternoon, but by the early evening he'd improved enough so we were able to do a procedure that corrected a problem with his heart. Looks like he'll be okay."

Could the music have turned things around for him? I was reminded of Mr. G and of my own case. Had there been a blossoming effect for John Peters, too, that had enabled him to stabilize?

John remained in the SICU for the remainder of that week, and I spent as much time with him as I could. I'd play a piece and he'd make up a poem, always beating time with his right hand. At one point, I played a Debussy prelude, "The Girl with the Flaxen Hair," originally written for the piano and that I'd arranged for guitar. He said, "It's like a delicate musical painting." It was a marvelous week.

A few months after he'd left the SICU, I heard from John. We'd created a close bond during his stay and we had a joyous reunion on the telephone. I told him there was something I wondered about. I knew from my own experience, both as a patient and as a SICU musician, that music, in the right circumstances, has great healing powers. My music had certainly acted on many different levels for him. As a bridge to developing a friendship with me through our shared love of music. As a way of accessing memories of people and occasions that were important to him. And as a pleasurable source of entertainment. Clearly many different regions of his brain had been activated, especially those relating to memory and emotions: the amygdala, nucleus accumbens, and hippocampus.

However, in his case I didn't think the music was the main intervention on that Friday. I had a hunch that he had really healed himself. My music was a spark, but it was all that time he'd spent reciting his own poetry that day that had fanned the flames and made the crucial difference. His poetry energized him, reminding him of something that had been so central to his life. To his soul. The music of his poetry stabilized him enough that the doctors were able to perform a life-saving procedure on his heart.

Interestingly, it turns out that scientists at the University of Exeter in the United Kingdom using fMRI brain scans have found that emotionally charged writing (both prose and poetry), as well as familiar writing, arouses those very same brain areas that respond to music that produces "shivers down the spine"— specifically, a brain region associated with reward. Interestingly, these neural patterns correlate with similar patterns of brain activity found during euphoria, sex, and the use of addictive drugs. John's poetry had really packed a punch that day.

Leonard Bernstein was a master at bringing out the poetry in music, as he did in his recording of Bach's *St. Matthew Passion*. Probably it was that as much as the brilliant rhythm, melodies, and harmonies that got through to me when I was slipping away to another world. It's all really quite poetic when you think about it.

One of the most influential figures to advance the cause of music therapy during the first two decades of the twentieth century was Eva Vescelius, a trained professional singer who sometimes performed concerts in hospitals and asylums.

She promoted music therapy through numerous publications and the National Therapeutic Society of New York which she founded in 1903.

Shortly before her death in 1918, Eva Vescelius provided a fascinating view of music therapy based on both age-old and contemporary concepts of health and disease. Vescelius felt that the object of music therapy was to return the sick person's discordant vibrations to harmonious ones. Vescelius asserted that the cures affected by music were based on the law of harmonious rhythmic vibration.*

—Jacqueline Schmidt Peters,
Music Therapy: An Introduction

*It's interesting to note that this can be viewed as akin to sympathetic vibrations, the harmonic phenomenon in which a formerly passive string or vibratory body responds to external vibrations to which it has a harmonic likeness.

14

Steppin' Out with My Baby

WORD GOT AROUND pretty quickly, after Wendy and I got home from the hospital, that I'd had a near-death experience. People started asking the question, "Did you see a white light?"

In the beginning, my response was, "I went into cardiac arrest right after the surgery and so I was still under the effects of anesthesia. Sorry, I have absolutely no recollection of seeing a white light."

That lasted for a couple of weeks. It was a boring answer. So for the next few weeks I tried something else.

"No white light, but I do have a distinct memory of feeling totally at peace because deep down inside I knew that I'd never have to answer another email or return another phone call."

Most people got the joke and laughed. But some people's eyes would open wide and they'd slowly nod their heads, as if I was confirming something for them. I decided I had to stop. It just wasn't right to joke about something so serious.

According to a study by Dr. Joel Funk, psychology professor at Plymouth State College in New Hampshire, around 50 percent of people who have had a near-death experience remember hearing music during their experience—usually "New Age synthesized music" with a "beautiful, floating sound."

The simple truth was that I really didn't have any recollection at all of the few minutes when I was clinically dead. I did have what Dr. Steven Ellman, a leading authority and author of eight books on physiology, psychoanalysis, and dreams, and a guitar friend, called dream-like visions, what I have always called coma dreams. We agreed that the first one I remembered, with me sprinting through a meadow in the Pacific Northwest, very likely happened in real time as they raced me on the gurney to the SICU. But there was nothing I could remember that resembled other people's near-death experiences.

It made me wonder what had been going on in my mind and body during those two minutes of cardiac arrest. The brain cannot function when the heart has stopped beating, and it typically shuts down within twenty to thirty seconds. There have been studies, though, that show that conscious awareness can continue after this time—patients who've reported watching themselves being resuscitated or hearing specific beeps from medical machines.

I consciously closed my eyes and took myself back to that moment. The instant I did, I saw Bed 11 during my Code Blue, a dozen or so doctors and nurses surrounding the bed. I saw my body on the bed, but I saw something else, too. A yellowish-white cloud hovering over me, the length of my body and about two feet thick. Flashes, like tiny lightning bolts, appeared here and there throughout the cloud. I saw it as my life force turning into electrical energy and leaving my body. This image was an extraordinarily powerful revelation, and it instantaneously imprinted itself in my brain. Now every time I think of myself during those first minutes in Bed 11, this exact picture, photographic in style, comes to mind. It's always there.

The image of the cloud, that moment of transition when life hangs in the balance, has been enormously helpful to me when I play in the SICU. It reminds me of the serious nature of what I do; that, while the SICU is primarily a place of healing, sometimes it is a place where death hovers closely.

I was feeling particularly carefree that crisp winter afternoon as I walked through the double doors. Maybe it was that sense of well-being that made me pause. Something about the patient in Bed 8 caught my eye.

He looked about forty, with black hair. He was on a ventilator but his head was turned all the way to the left, a strange redness circling his mouth. His legs were angled strangely; knees out, feet touching. There was something else that I couldn't quite pinpoint. As if there was a dark aura in the space around him.

After a few seconds, I continued on and started with the day as usual, studying each patient's numbers on the main computer monitor, following that with my stroll through the unit while playing. The SICU was full today. The patient in Bed 6, a man in his eighties with white, close-cropped hair and a gaunt face, was still there. In two weeks I'd never once seen his eyes open. He breathed through a tube because of a tracheotomy. Each time I played, his vital signs showed clear improvement, the only sign the music was having its healing effect.

To the left, in Bed 5, Mary, a small woman in her nineties, with gray hair in a pixie cut and bright blue eyes, was sitting up and conversing with a woman and man. They looked my way several times as I played, smiling.

To the right the patient in Bed 7 was moving his feet in time to the music. Gershwin's "Embraceable You" elicited big smiles and thumbs-up from the three at Bed 5 and, finally, a discernable reaction from the man in Bed 6. Eyes still closed, his left hand rose a few inches. He was playing air guitar! I could swear he was doing a vibrato, the shake of the hand that puts some spin on a note. The kind of day I love.

Toward the end of the session, everything changed. I heard voices and rapid footsteps. Fast movement in the SICU is never a good sign. I turned my head and saw two nurses hurry toward Bed 8. After a minute, one of them came back out from behind the curtain, and I asked what was happening. Without looking up, she said, "Not responsive."

In less than a minute, a team of doctors, nurses, and respiratory therapists surrounded the bed. Someone wheeled the red crash cart from the far end of the unit. Code Blue. Those words always send a chill down my spine. It means the patient requires immediate resuscitation. If not, he will die. I was a Code Blue on that first night.

I was sitting about three feet away from the main computer monitor. I looked over and saw the patient's heart rate was 52.

For the next twenty minutes, as I tried to focus on my music, I watched it fall to zero.

I would normally stay longer in situations like this, at least to help calm the staff, but I had a concert that night. I put on my coat and pulled the straps of the guitar case over my shoulders. A nurse had just come on duty, and I overheard her speaking in hushed tones with an intern. "The patient attempted suicide, he shot himself in the mouth. Surgery was this morning. Complications."

I was stunned. That explained the discoloration around his mouth and why his head was tilted at an odd angle. And perhaps why I felt such a strange energy around him. I wondered about the reasons behind his failed attempt. Maybe at the last possible second he wanted to live and his hand moved. Or someone surprised him in the act, startled him, and his hand moved. Or, he'd bungled it, was conscious of that, and whatever pain led him to the attempt was now even more excruciating.

These thoughts flooded my mind as I made my way past Bed 8. The Code Blue team was still in place. Dr. McMillen was in charge, looking exactly as Wendy described when he was there at my Code Blue—a general leading a battle. I saw Scott Gould, the chief PA, doing manual chest compressions, very fast and hard, at least one hundred a minute. I looked up at the computer monitor over the bed. The lines on the screen were still flat.

It was like watching a scene in a movie. More staff gathered near the bed until McMillen turned and, with a voice like a bullhorn, ordered everyone nonessential to leave. I turned and walked out the double doors.

I hardly slept that weekend. I had witnessed what Wendy saw when she walked into the SICU and saw me in a Code

Blue. I understood now why she said it was the most terrifying moment of her life. I would have to wait until Monday to learn the answer to the question tugging at me: Did they save him? Did they pull him back?

My heart was beating fast as I walked into the SICU on Monday. The curtain was pulled in front of Bed 8. I stopped and peered through a small opening.

The patient was there, still hooked up to the ventilator, but now his face looked peaceful. His heart rate was 98; blood pressure was 132/69. Good numbers, really good since they'd been 0 the last time I saw them. I felt exuberance. And pride. I was very proud of this team I'd been allowed to be part of, the team that had saved me, and had now saved this poor man.

My friend June, one of the unit secretaries, was sitting at a computer terminal. Barely able to control my excitement, I said, "June, I can't *believe* they saved the guy in Bed 8! I was here on Friday afternoon, I was sure he was gone when I left!" June just looked at me, expressionless. In the fraction of a second before she spoke, I knew.

"He's dead, Andrew. Brain dead. They signed the death certificate Friday night. The machines are keeping the body alive so they can harvest the organs."

June showed no emotion, but she's not a cold person. You adapt in the SICU. You have to. I hadn't gotten to that level yet, though, and the emotions churned through me. I made a quick decision.

"I'm going to play for him."

June looked puzzled. "Why? He's dead."

"I don't care, he only has a few hours left on earth in this form. He deserves a farewell."

A few minutes later, I was sitting next to the inert body of a man. I decided to play the *First Cello Suite* by Bach, the sublime music I'd played for John Peters and so many others in the past two years. It had never failed to have a positive effect. But as soon as I played the first note, I knew I needed to make a change. I couldn't have a positive effect anymore. I couldn't reach him. I had to find some balance or the wrenching drama of the SICU would overwhelm me.

It was clear that I had to be a medical musician in the truest meaning of the word *medical*. Take the opportunity to learn, to increase my understanding of the science of medicine, and get better at it.

So, I'd honor this man's passing and play for him. Right brain. And I'd observe the effect of playing for a patient who is brain dead. Left brain. I stepped off the emotional roller coaster and it calmed me.

For twenty minutes, I played his farewell music and kept my eye on the computer monitor. The music had no effect at all. His heart rate remained constant at 98, his blood pressure at 132/69. Oxygenation, respiration, even the waveforms had a perfect continuity. Machines were keeping the cells alive. It reminded me that sometimes the sickest patients in the SICU have the best vital signs—because they're being helped by multiple machines. This man was brain dead. He'd had a catastrophic brain injury and now had no brain function at all. I was playing for a dead man. There was no "him" there anymore. It was time to play for life.

I walked over to Bed 5. When Mary saw me come through the curtain, her face lit up. With her radiant expression, clear blue eyes, and silvery hair, she looked like an angel. Her daughter and son-in-law were at her side again.

Would she like some more Gershwin?

"Yes!"

I began the intro to "They Can't Take That Away from Me." Mary lay back on the pillow, and, with her eyes shut tight, began conducting every beat with both hands. I followed her lead.

"Look," her daughter said. She was pointing at the computer monitor. "That's just what the doctor wanted!" When I'd started playing her heart rate was 92, and now it was 97. It seemed odd—I would have thought they'd want to see the number get lower.

I played the last chord, and Mary said, "More! Do you know 'Steppin' Out with My Baby'?" I did indeed—a cheerful Irving Berlin tune popularized by Fred Astaire.

"That was my mother and father's favorite song to dance to," said her daughter. She reached into her bag, took out a Valentine's Day card, and, handing it to her mother, said, "Mom, look what I brought you." Mary took the card. It was the last Valentine's Day card her husband, who'd died a year ago, had given her. She smiled and pressed it to her heart. Tomorrow was Valentine's Day.

I began to play. Closing her eyes, Mary once again kept time, now with just one hand, holding the card and all its memories with the other, with her favorite music also reaching into the deepest part of a memory that made her so happy and content, even lying in a hospital bed. She was moving in the bed— perhaps dancing in body and mind with her beloved husband. I had seen this before, the way music connected people to their memories. But we could see she was growing tired. The hand keeping the beat slowed and finally dropped onto the Valentine, and with a sweet smile Mary floated off to sleep.

Two days later I was back and started the session with my usual walk through the unit to see all the patients. Mary, who'd told me on Monday how much she'd wanted to go home, was no longer in Bed 5. I wondered if she'd gone to Step-Down or directly to a regular room. Maybe she'd even been well enough to go home.

It was one of those pleasantly uneventful days. No drama of any kind. That day I played more for the staff than the patients. Their favorites—Bach's "Jesu, Joy of Man's Desiring" and the Beatles song "Yesterday." And a dreamy Filipino ballad, "Dahil sa Isang Bulaklak" ("Because of a Flower"), that I'd arranged for nurses Madelene and Rosievic. It reminded them of home. Soon it was time to go. I was packing the guitar and music when Sandy, the nurse practitioner, walked over to me.

"Andrew, glad I caught you before you left. Two things. First, I know you played for one of my patients on Monday, the elderly woman in Bed 5. I was watching. I'm happy you did. I'm sorry to have to tell you this but later that evening she died of heart failure. Her daughter and son-in-law were with her at the end. I thought you'd want to know."

I nodded, sadly. That must have been why they'd been excited when her heart rate went up. There'd been hope that her heart was getting better.

In just a few short days I'd experienced death twice in the SICU. The first, a man whose spirit had been crushed and died all alone. The second, a woman who clearly had lived a full life, and died surrounded by her loving family.

I looked over at Bed 5, empty now. They say that at the end it is your family that is most important to help make the transition. And Mary had something else at the end that she loved. Music. She'd gotten the chance for one more dance. She had stepped out with her baby in her heart and her little girl at her side.

I turned to go, but Sandy had something else to tell me.

"I just took a phone call from a man who was a patient in Bed 7 last November, Bob Harper. You played at his bedside for two weeks after he coded. He and his family remembered you, and they want you to play at his daughter's wedding in October."

Perfect timing. I had just experienced two deaths; there is nothing more life affirming than a wedding.

A few months later, as I listened to Emily and Matt speak their wedding vows, I looked at Bob Harper, sitting in the front row just a few feet away. A man who almost died in the SICU, a man I played for and helped heal. I got misty-eyed. It all came home. A wedding. I was playing for something very precious, and very fragile. I was playing for life.

During World War II, numerous organizations, including the Musicians Emergency Fund, the Hospitalized Veterans Music Service, Sigma Alpha Iota, Mu Phi Epsilon, the American Red Cross, and Delta Omicron, provided musicians to Veterans Administration hospitals and later to state institutions. These volunteers assisted hospital staff in organizing music programs for patients.

By the conclusion of World War II, many U.S. medical facilities, recognizing the value of music as therapy, employed music programs to assist in the physical and mental rehabilitation of returning soldiers.

—**Davis, Gfeller, and Thaut,**
An Introduction to Music Therapy—
Theory and Practice

15

The Memory of All That

ERNIE HARBURG HAD HIRED me to play guitar for Deena during her recuperation in their East Village apartment. They both thought the music I had provided in the SICU had been an integral part of her recovery. Ernie suggested a fee, a good one, and when I thanked him for the offer he laughed. "Yip will be paying you!" "Over the Rainbow" and many other Yip Harburg songs had been earning substantial royalties ever since he wrote them. I loved the thought that I'd be working for Yip Harburg.

When I got off the phone, I felt an immediate compulsion to try and play at least *one* Gershwin song for Deena from memory. After all, Ernie had known George Gershwin when he was a little boy, and Deena had been very close to Ira Gershwin late in his life. It had been almost a year since I'd given up the effort to memorize music but I committed to it once again. My personal favorite Gershwin song was "Embraceable You" and I set to work immediately.

Trying to memorize music was still torture. I could get a few measures down and then five minutes later they were gone. Yet again I'd close my eyes and see blank paper instead of notes on the page.

But it was summer, and I had the time, so I spent hours a day working on just that one song. By the end of the first week, a few measures of music finally stayed in my head, and in a few more days, more imprinted without disappearing. For the first time, I allowed myself some hope—maybe my memory loss was not permanent after all.

By the end of the second week, I could make it all the way to the end, although with nowhere near the fluency I'd had before. I was now cautiously optimistic.

It was time for me to play for Deena. After exchanging warm greetings, I told her I had something special to play. I made it all the way through to the end. No mistakes. When I finished, Deena was beaming, even more excited by the performance from memory than I was. We shared a wonderful hour together of music and conversation.

However, when I left I had an unsettled feeling. I wondered what would happen if I didn't spend the next few days working on the song. I feared it would vanish completely from my memory.

It did.

I decided I couldn't spend weeks at a time memorizing one song if it wasn't going to stick. I'd fully adjusted to reading sheet music and things were fine that way—in the SICU and in other music work I was doing. I accepted, again, that I'd always carry with me my black bag, heavy with folders of music, and my music stand. That's just the way it would be.

Every September, the Louis Armstrong Center for Music and Medicine holds an annual fund-raiser, which includes the "What a Wonderful World" award ceremony, the name taken from the song most associated with Armstrong. Each year three people are chosen to receive the award: a famous musician with a connection to medicine, a doctor or nurse from Beth Israel who was involved with music, and a patient, or former patient, also involved in some way with music. This year the musician would be Levon Helm, formerly the drummer and singer with the '60s rock band The Band. After The Band broke up Levon had continued doing his own music. In 1998, he'd been diagnosed with throat cancer and had lost his ability to sing for years, but by 2004, with the cancer in remission, he was singing again. Dr. McMillen and I were also chosen to receive the award. For months Wendy and I were as excited as could be. We were huge fans of both Levon Helm and The Band.

It was a fantastic evening. Levon spoke first, making brief remarks about how grateful he was for the award. McMillen came next and spent his time mostly talking about me. That's his style. He was proud of having said yes to my request to play in the SICU and he loved talking about others.

I spoke last, thanking McMillen and Loewy for allowing me to return to the SICU, and then continuing with a nutshell version of the crux of the story—how Wendy and Bach had helped my doctors and nurses save my life.

I finished with these words:

"The best lesson a young musician can have is to listen to a great performer. In September 1969, when I was seventeen years old, I heard a song on the radio. What I loved most was the sound of the singer. Spanish musicians have a name for it. *Cante jondo.* It means 'deep singing.' I had no idea back then that forty-two years later I'd be accepting a wonderful award like this, and I'd tell the audience that the song was 'The Night They Drove Old Dixie Down,' the band was The Band, and the singer was Levon Helm." I turned. "Levon, thank you for giving me such a great lesson then in how to make music, and for all the lessons and music you've given the world throughout your life."

Wendy and my friends in the audience told me that, from the moment he arrived, Levon had looked tired and pale, but as I spoke and he saw where it was going he came to life and was beaming at the end. When I finished, I went over to him and we hugged. He and I bonded that night. There is a picture of the two of us that I will always cherish.

What no one outside his inner circle knew that night was that the cancer had returned. He would die seven months later, to the day.

The next morning I received a phone call from Levon's manager, Barbara O'Brien. The first thing she said was that Levon had loved the evening and what he enjoyed most was that I'd mentioned him in the same sentence with J. S. Bach! She went on to tell me about the weekly Saturday night concerts, the Midnight Rambles that Levon had in his home-studio in Woodstock. Started in 2003 to pay his medical bills, he'd kept them going because they were so successful. I knew people came from all over the world for them—they were always sold out.

The guest artist scheduled for the following week had just canceled and Levon wanted to know if I would like to step in. I instantly agreed, but inside I was terrified. I knew the guest artists were often famous musicians. Could I pull it off? I hadn't played a solo concert for over two years.

I asked Wendy to join me and sing a couple of songs with my accompaniment. She was delighted, and she certainly deserved the spotlight. It would also relieve the pressure on me, less solo time to fill.

Once again, I felt compelled to try to memorize something. Barbara had said I could play anything I wanted but they preferred American music. Gershwin music was classic American music. I'd try and get "Embraceable You" back in my head and, feeling that Levon, a proud Southerner, would especially enjoy it, I decided to take a crack at "Summertime," from *Porgy and Bess*, once a staple of my repertoire. I did have one other tune to play from memory, the Beatles song, "Here Comes the Sun," one of the few pieces that had stayed in my hippocampus and, although not American, it was close enough. Levon was good friends with, and had done concerts with, Ringo Starr. I'd open with that.

I practiced relentlessly to get the notes into my head, constantly on the edge of panic. Fortunately, both Gershwin tunes started to click. I decided to be bolder: I would try to restore my favorite set closer, the Beatles' "Norwegian Wood." If I was going to fall on my face, I might as well do it big-time. I was still working on the songs right up to the final half hour I spent in the green-room, getting ready to go onstage.

When I walked out on that stage the energy from the packed house of two hundred music lovers from all over the world hit me like a bolt of electricity. Barbara O'Brien gave a moving introduction, briefly telling the audience how Levon and I had met ten days before. "Here Comes the Sun," George Harrison's masterpiece, had its usual galvanizing effect. The two Gershwin numbers got the same enthusiastic reaction. I made it through with every note intact and tried not to show the utter relief on my face as I stood for the applause. I then told the story about Wendy's intuition during the coma and how her decision to play Bach's music saved my life. The audience had no idea she was nearby, and when I introduced her and said she'd join me on-stage she was greeted with thunderous applause. She sang beautifully, starting with the spiritual "Goin' Home," followed by another of her favorites, "Black Is the Color of My True Love's Hair." I played a few more solos, reading them, and finished the set by playing "Norwegian Wood" from memory. The applause flowed through every cell in my body.

When Levon and his eleven-piece band took the stage, Barbara offered me a seat at the side, two feet from Levon's drum kit. His playing dazzled me. I was mesmerized from the first down-beat. His beat was rock steady, the cross-rhythms shimmered, and the part he created fit the song like a glove. There is a special name for that kind of playing: "song drummer." His band played a two-and-a-half-hour set, and I never left my spot for a second. At one point, I realized that it was as great a music lesson as the one I'd had with Andrés Segovia over thirty years before.

When the last encore was played he introduced each member of his band and then to my surprise and delight he turned to me and did the same. He gave me a bear hug and whispered in my ear, "Great set, man!" That was the last time I saw him.

The next day I awoke to a strange sensation in my head. It literally felt as if my brain was tingling. On a whim I took out my favorite Bach fugue, the so-called Fiddle Fugue, a six-minute piece that I couldn't play in public because it is so long and a guitarist can't turn pages with one hand like a pianist can. I sat down and started playing the compact opening theme, four repeated notes that blossom into a complex and ingenious piece of music.

Fifty-five minutes later, every note of this great work of art was back in my memory. I could play it all the way through without the printed page, which I did three times in a row. I was absolutely flabbergasted, and completely bewildered. I had never before been able to memorize something that difficult in that short a time. And when I closed my eyes I didn't see a blank piece of paper. I saw the notes, just like I used to before I lost my memory. Could it be true? Did I dare hope that the damage had finally healed?

I had a new steady gig then at a place called Alouette, a French bistro near where I lived. It was the first time in my four decades as a musician in New York City that I could walk to work. The first thing I played that night was the fugue. It was still intact. A musician friend and neighbor, the composer Nancy Ford, was there for dinner, and when I finished playing she remarked that she'd never heard me sound so good, and we'd been friends for thirty years. Even some of the waiters came over and commented that there was a noticeable difference.

Something else was happening, as well. The only way I could describe it is to say that my music brain was functioning much faster now. Later in the evening, I played the fugue again, and I had a memory lapse halfway through. There is a term "going off the rails." For musicians, it means you get lost and can't find your way back to the right spot. It's why playing Bach from memory can be so intimidating: the music is so complex that it's easy to get lost and sometimes you have to just start over from the beginning. But now, for the first time in my life, I could spot an entry point either just before or just after the lost notes and my fingers flew there. I was amazed and said to myself, "How did you just do that?" There was another sensation that happened all through the evening when I read the music of other pieces: it now felt like I was "inside" the music. In comparison, it seemed like everything I'd done before had been from the outside looking in. It was all quite cool but also very freaky—and even a bit scary. It actually reminded me of my coma dreams. Everything was so vivid, and, at the same time, dreamlike.

One of the regulars, and by now a friend, Dr. Phil Brotman, was sitting at the table right next to me. He and Judy Kellersberger, a songwriter, came nearly every week to hear me. Phil is not a musician. He started out as a physicist and then became a pioneer in the field of biofeedback, a treatment technique in which people are taught to improve their health by monitoring signals given off by their own bodies. Phil loves music as much as anyone I've ever met and has a highly discriminating ear for music and sound. He told me that not only did he hear a difference in my playing, but he'd been hearing incremental improvements in my playing for months and had wondered if it had to do with my brain damage healing. When he left that night, he said he'd talk to a friend of his, Dr. Kamran Fallahpour, a clinical psychologist/neuroscientist who specialized in brain scans.

In the meantime, I was absorbing pieces into my memory every day like a sponge, and having a fantastic time playing old pieces, and hearing new things in them, the way melodies interacted, how harmonies colored the sound in ways I hadn't noticed before, and different accents implicit in the rhythms that hadn't stood out that way previously.

At the beginning of the next week, as I took Dolly and Paco to the dog run in Riverside Park, I bumped into someone I knew, a retired surgeon who'd done a fellowship in neurosurgery. I told him everything that was happening.

When I finished, he remained silent for a few moments as we walked. He finally said, "Okay, I'm pretty sure I know now what's going on. You've been experiencing neuroplasticity of the brain. You thought in the beginning that the brain cells were destroyed and couldn't regenerate. You were wrong: the neural pathways were damaged, but not destroyed. When your head hurt so much in the beginning when you got home from the hospital and you played the Bach Sarabande, that was your brain creating a workaround, making new connections to other parts of the brain so you could at least play and read music. But the memory area was too badly damaged to function. However, because you kept playing, even that repaired. You are experiencing increased neurological function, you hear more and memorize faster, because the brain doesn't discard a workaround it has created. It blends it into the repaired nerve network." He smiled and said, "The computer analogy is that you just got a faster processor and more memory. You now have Music Brain 2.0. Congratulations."

Two things happened when he finished that explanation. First, I didn't feel like some freaky thing was happening to me. It wasn't like a coma dream anymore. It was reality. The next thought was—I've got to find out more about this from a medical and scientific perspective.

A friend suggested I contact Dr. Oliver Sacks. A great idea, as I was feeling like an Oliver Sacks patient at this point. In the middle of the night, I sent a detailed email. Just hours later, I received a reply from his longtime editor, Kate Edgar. She and Dr. Sacks had read my account, and he suggested I contact the person who'd been his primary consultant in the field of music therapy for the past twenty-five years, Dr. Connie Tomaino.

As soon as I finished reading, I Googled her name, and in just a few seconds I made an astonishing discovery. It had been thirty-five years, but as they say, you can always tell from the eyes. I knew Connie Tomaino. She was my schoolmate from Stony Brook University, the student who had been on fire with her dream of becoming a music therapist. In 1995, she and Sacks had cofounded the Institute for Music and Neurologic Function, located at a skilled nursing subacute rehabilitation center in the Bronx, part of Beth Abraham, the hospital where Sacks worked in the '60s and '70s. Tomaino came to Beth Abraham in 1980 and is executive director of the institute. Clearly she'd lived her dream, in spades.

I called her immediately and was delighted that within seconds she remembered our conversation as well as I had. We had a college reunion on the phone and a few weeks later I was on the 2 train heading up to the Bronx to meet her. She gave me a tour of the facility she'd created with Sacks and then we went to her office for the first of three meetings we had that month.

She confirmed everything that my friend the surgeon had deduced about my neurological situation. I mentioned to her that I'd never bothered seeing a neurologist because I had thought brain damage was permanent. She laughed.

"Lucky you didn't," she said, "because they probably would have told you that you couldn't do what you did!" She went on: "You didn't forget any of that music, it was just that the connections, the nerve networks, had been badly damaged. And as luck, or fate, or whatever it was would have it, playing in the SICU was the most perfect rehab you could ever have had. It had all the right ingredients: repetition, you were there three days a week, intensity—nothing could have been more intense for you than playing in a SICU, a room of life and death where you yourself almost died—and a focus on healing others and not yourself. You never had to judge your own progress and so never risked getting frustrated to the point where you might have quit. If you hadn't gone back to the SICU your brain might still have healed and the music memory might have returned but it would have taken years longer, at least five to ten in my experience. However, in my opinion, and I've seen many cases like this over the years, if you hadn't played in the SICU it is very likely that you would have quit music altogether in the first year out of sheer frustration."

Tomaino loved the Music Brain 2.0 computer analogy. "Sure, by helping to heal others you defragged your hard drive!"

Dr. Phil, my Alouette friend, came through for me. He directed me to Dr. Kamran Fallahpour. Fallahpour, who was born in Iran and moved to the United States in the early '80s, is a decade younger than me.

He suggested we do two types of scans of my brain: a specific type of MRI (magnetic resonance imaging), the scan commonly used to investigate the anatomy and physiology in order to make diagnoses for many different kinds of diseases and injuries; and a qEEG (quantitative electroencephalography), a scan that looks at the brain's electrical activity and its function rather than structure. I would also have a neuropsychological screening to evaluate various cognitive functions such as memory, attention, executive functions, and verbal fluency and motor skills.

The MRI would be done by a colleague of Fallahpour's, Dr. Michael Lipton, associate director of the Gruss Magnetic Resonance Research Center at Albert Einstein College of Medicine. We were hoping to see if we could tell how my brain—and specifically those parts of the brain associated with memory— rewired after the trauma.

The results of the MRI simply showed that my brain was normal. We didn't have a scan to compare it to before, but we already knew it wasn't functioning properly following the cardiac arrest, ischemia, and oxygen shortage because I had been unable to play from memory or relearn new music.

Fallahpour did the qEEG himself and it did reveal something that helped to explain the new changes in my music brain. As he said, "The qEEG refers to a functional brain mapping procedure that allows measurement of the brain's electrical activity and then comparison to established norms. It differs from MRIs and CAT scans that look at the brain's anatomy by examining possible structural abnormalities. In most traumatic brain injury cases, such as yours, it can be difficult to identify structural abnormalities, and so a procedure such as qEEG may be more useful as it will identify areas of functional disturbance even when the structure of the brain seems intact. A good analogy would be software issues versus hardware issues."

After conducting a qEEG, a report can then be generated that allows for comparison of a patient's brain activity to established norms and, through statistical and numeric values, indicates how far from the norm a patient's data fall. Color-coded brain maps—topographies—give a visual representation of the data and can highlight specific regions in the brain that show disturbance.

After analyzing my results, Fallahpour said he'd expected to see a lot more disturbance in my brain map given the magnitude of injury I'd had. He'd thought he might see areas of disturbance in both brain functions and cognition. Over the years he'd done more than a thousand brain maps of people in New York, including dozens and dozens of people with brain injury and mine, he said, was one of the healthiest results he'd seen, given the history. Again, he explained, we didn't have a pre-injury qEEG to compare it to, but we did have other comparisons to use—the consensus of opinion from people who had heard me play for years that there was a noticeable decline after the coma, then a steady improvement in my playing, and finally the stunning difference I felt in my musical abilities now after almost fifty years of playing the guitar.

Moreover, in addition to the qEEG, Fallahpour carried out a neurocognitive battery to screen for any areas of dysfunction in my cognitive functions, testing at least five major networks in the brain, including memory (memory recall and recognition), attention, executive functions, verbal fluency, and motor control. The results, he said, were pretty much normal, meaning that my cognitive function tested within the norms. Here was further confirmation that somehow my damaged brain had rearranged and retrained itself.

The question I had for Fallahpour was simple: Did he agree with Tomaino's assessment that the SICU was the best possible rehab I could have had?

He paused, then nodded his head. "Yes, I think by committing yourself to playing in the SICU you forced your brain to rewire. The consistent and deliberate exercise every day of what you had to do to become what you call a medical musician, the constant auditory attention, the intense thinking as you watched the patients' responses and the changes, or lack of changes, in the vital signs monitors over their beds, your constant awareness of all the sounds surrounding you so you could be attuned to other needs should an emergency like a Code Blue arise, and, very importantly, making sure all your fine motor functions were at their best to guide you in making soothing and healing music for your patients—all these factors combined to force different parts of your brain to make new connections, to talk to each other. There is a famous saying in the field of neuroscience: neurons that fire together, wire together. Put it all together and that's what happened. There is plenty of evidence and a number of studies that point to the idea that musical training makes meaningful changes in both brain structure and function."

Fallahpour paused again, and smiled. "Yes, you did repair your own brain, and gave yourself an upgrade at the same time."

I'd gone back to the SICU to avoid survivor's guilt and to give thanks for a great gift after having my life saved. I stayed because I found I loved this new experience of helping and healing others through music.

I wound up healing myself, as well.

Probably the most important leader in the field of music therapy during the formative years of NAMT was E. Thayer Gaston (1901–1971).

As Chairman of the Music Education department at the University of Kansas, he championed the cause of music therapy during the decades of the 1940s, 50s, and 60s.

In collaboration with the renowned Menninger Clinic, a facility in Topeka, Kansas, that specialized in the treatment of mental disorders, he established the first internship-training site in the United States.

In addition, Gaston established the first graduate music therapy program in the U.S. at the University of Kansas.* His "insatiable thirst" for knowledge, dedication to scholarship and unquestioned integrity led to his pre-eminent position in the field and many of his associates referred to him as the "father of music therapy."

—Davis, Gfeller, and Thaut,
An Introduction to Music Therapy—
Theory and Practice

*The University of Kansas continues to have a thriving music education and music therapy program. E. Thayer Gaston would have been proud.

16

Wild Horses

IT WAS A WEDNESDAY AFTERNOON. As soon as I entered the SICU a nurse told me the patient in Bed 4 was in crisis again. I pulled my guitar out of its case, grabbed a book of music, and hurried toward his bed.

His name was Elliott Bernerd, but I thought of him as my English patient, as he was here from the United Kingdom. He'd come to Beth Israel for minor abdominal surgery to repair a hernia and, unfortunately, had aspirated at the end of the operation. Undetected stomach contents had made their way into his lungs, a surgeon's worst nightmare, and a potentially fatal turn of events. It was a mad dash on a gurney from the OR to the SICU and, like me, he'd been put into a medically induced coma. His situation was highly critical from the very beginning.

He'd been here a week now, and I'd played at his bedside several times, spending as much time with him as I could, hoping to find a way to get through to him. His mother Trudie, and David, who I'd guessed to be a family member but was actually Elliott's assistant, both sat by his side every day. I'd gotten to know them well as I played music they said he loved—classical music, the old standards, and especially Gershwin. Trudie had told me Elliott always played Gershwin music on his stereo at dinner.

But each day his condition had worsened. At the end of the week, there was an entire day when it was touch and go. Dr. Asaf Gave, the attending physician, struggled for over ten hours to keep oxygenation levels up, a complicated procedure requiring great medical skill. If Gave hadn't been so adept, the patient would have died.

As I drew close to Bed 4, I had a feeling that death was imminent now. I'd seen this scenario before. Elliott was completely unresponsive—no movement of any kind, and his face had an ashen pallor. His heart rate and blood pressure were already below the normal range, and I watched the numbers steadily descend on the monitor. I looked at the resident, the PA, and the nurses standing at the bedside, and I saw great concern in their eyes. Trudie kept walking around the bed, shaking her hands. She was talking to herself, praying quietly.

I pulled up a chair and looked at this man who had survived jaw cancer eleven years earlier, who hadn't let the ensuing disfiguration get in the way of his life. Surely something could reach that fighting spirit in him. I had the Rolling Stones songbook in my hand. David had mentioned to me that Elliott loved their music. Trudie had confirmed that there was a portrait of Mick Jagger in his London home. I'd gone out and bought a book of all their songs the next day.

I knew how crucial the choice of music had been when Wendy clicked on the first track on my iPod playlist. By good fortune, she had played the *St. Matthew Passion*, my favorite music, and its familiarity and power had given my body the energy it so desperately needed.

I also sensed, as Wendy had, that something had to happen right now or it would be too late for my English patient. I racked my brain trying to think which song might have a chance of making the difference between life and death.

As it turned out, I didn't think of it. I heard it. An acoustic guitar chord rang out in my head, echoed by a lead guitar's delicate filigree of descending notes in response. I wanted Elliott to feel that it wasn't time to leave his mother, his daughters and grandchildren, his friends. His life. I wanted him to feel that wild horses couldn't drag him away.

I opened the book to "Wild Horses" and starting played that opening chord and the filigree of notes that followed. When the melody began, I did my best to make my guitar sing like Jagger. I wanted Elliott to hear it all, to see those wild horses.

Within less than a minute, his completely unresponsive body showed signs of life. His brow furrowed and, although his eyes were still closed, his eyelids began to narrow, almost as if he was squinting, deep in thought.

"Wild Horses" is a long song, and I played it twice. We all saw it really was getting through. He was returning to this world. The numbers on the computer monitor leveled off for a while and then started to rise. The fear gripping Trudie's face ebbed away. David looked back and forth at Elliott, at me, and at the Rolling Stones songbook on my music stand. His expression of deep concern morphed into a smile. I think he already knew he'd done something he'd remember for the rest of his life. He'd told me about Elliott's love for the Stones. He'd given me the key.

By the end of that hour, "Ruby Tuesday," "As Tears Go By," "Brown Sugar," and others had followed those wild horses, and it was clear to everyone that Elliott was back. Just as in my case three years earlier, there were no more crises and he never regressed. The doctors kept him in the coma for another week to be safe, gradually weaning him off the drugs and ventilator.

In the days after Elliott awoke from the coma, I saw him look depressed just once. He was on a gurney ready to go to the Radiology Department when the telephone near me rang. A nurse answered, and then told the transporter to wait. The radiation unit needed another ten minutes. I was watching Elliott's face when his nurse gave him the news. A seemingly small thing, but he'd been through so much. He turned his head away, looking terribly downcast. I hatched a plan.

When the phone rang again giving the okay, the gurney started moving toward me. I waited until he was about three feet away, then started playing, loud as I could, the famous opening guitar riff from the Stones classic "(I Can't Get No) Satisfaction." Elliott went from zero to sixty in a millisecond. With a huge grin from ear to ear, he kicked the white hospital blanket into the air with his right leg, then pumped both arms up, high in the air, to the beat. The entire SICU transformed into a rock concert. Practically every doctor, nurse, and patient began to smile and laugh, some swaying to the beat, and the whole place soared with Elliott's exuberant energy. I saw an elderly woman in Bed 6, who hadn't smiled in three weeks, beaming, her eyes shining.

This is what music and joy can do for critically ill patients in a surgical intensive care unit. Watching him roll past me, I understood more than ever why once music ignited his spirit in that coma, he was able to reach up and grab back his life. And then he could do something he'd done all his life: use his energy to help others.

I learned much later, after he left the hospital, that Elliott is a well-known British businessman and patron of the arts—a former chairman of the London Philharmonic Orchestra and chairman of the Southbank Centre, which incorporates the Royal Festival Hall, Europe's largest center for the arts. His philanthropy has supported music, and he has been a major donor for medical research, especially via the THANC Foundation, a foundation dedicated to advanced research for thyroid, head, and neck cancer, and as chairman of Saving Faces—The Facial Surgery Research Foundation, the only charity in the United Kingdom solely dedicated to the worldwide reduction of facial injuries and diseases.

As has been the case throughout the millennia, music and musicians need financial support in order to survive. Centuries ago, in Europe, the Church and wealthy patrons like the Medici family of Florence provided that support. Bach's famous Goldberg Variations resulted from a commission from Count Hermann Karl von Keyserlingk, the Russian ambassador to the Saxon court, a major patron of the arts. I know from many people in the field of Music & Medicine today that if it weren't for donors and patrons, they would not be able to do what they do.

Currently, our health care systems do not support music as a medical modality to the extent they could. Music in medicine is a noninvasive approach without side effects that does as good a job—if not better—as many very expensive and invasive drugs and technologies, many of which have terrible and long-lasting side effects. However, music therapy is not yet included as a covered service under many public and private insurance plans, which immediately limits its availability to patients as a treatment option. If a patient's insurance will not reimburse for services, then most patients will not be able to receive those services. It's as simple as that. According to Judy Simpson, director of government relations for the American Music Therapy Association, the AMTA "has initiated several projects that have contributed to increasing the percentage of music therapy services receiving reimbursement" and estimates that approximately 20 percent of music therapists currently receive some form of third-party reimbursement. However, reimbursement is not a given. Usually, it occurs on a "case-by-case basis when the therapist communicates with case managers and receives pre-approval for services. This process often requires that the therapist provide a physician's referral, supportive research, and evidence of the medical or behavioral necessity of music therapy for that particular client." In other words, it's a lot of paperwork. Something needs to change so that insurance companies will consistently include music therapy as a covered service. I hope my work at Beth Israel will be part of that change.

In the time I've played in the SICU, I've seen music help to soothe and heal hundreds of patients directly. I've also seen the power of music to soothe and heal patients indirectly, by helping the people the patients rely on so much—their family and friends and the whole medical team, all the people that make such a difference in the outcomes of every patient.

There is no such thing as a panacea in medicine, or in medical music. However, a healing environment that includes music will provide a better chance at the best possible medical outcome. Logic indicates that the more therapeutic music is available in a critical care unit, the greater the chance that seemingly miraculous events will occur more frequently.

I was playing one winter's night at Alouette, my favorite little bistro. Two couples were sitting at a nearby table, and I could tell they were listening intently to my music all through the evening. One of the men, elderly, with very short cropped gray hair, was sitting in a wheelchair. When they all got up to leave, this man's wife came over to talk to me. She was in her seventies, with piercing blue eyes and a friendly smile. She introduced herself as Barbara Wilson Lloyd and told me that the dinner party that evening had been to celebrate her husband David's ninety-first birthday. She and David were retired musicians, Barbara a classical bass player, and David a singer. She mentioned that she'd been the principal bassist and orchestral contractor for forty years for Musica Sacra, a highly regarded ensemble, the longest continuously performing professional chorus in New York. David had had a long and illustrious career as a professional classical stage singer. She'd come over to tell me how much they'd enjoyed my Bach playing. I felt especially honored by this; Musica Sacra was renowned for its performances of Bach's cantatas, oratorios, and passions.

I saw Barbara again a week later but this time David was not with her. She told me the dinner the previous week was just before he had major brain surgery for an undiagnosed head injury sustained decades earlier. Some brain injuries can take many years to emerge and do their damage, and the future for him was very uncertain. She looked exhausted. Over the next few weeks she'd come occasionally for a late supper after spending a day with David in the hospital. One night she came in, walked over to me, and said that David had just been transferred to a rehabilitation facility on the East Side. She asked if I would take a break later and join her when she was having dessert.

She told me that the situation with David was bleak. However, she needed to relax her mind and not dwell on it. She'd heard a little bit from the owners of Alouette that I'd been through a very unusual medical experience. "They didn't tell me much but said it had something to do with music; would you mind telling me the story?"

So I told her a short version of the story and when I got to the part about the *St. Matthew Passion* I mentioned that the recording was the 1962 version conducted by Leonard Bernstein. Every time I've told this part of the story to a musician who knows that masterpiece, there is the same reaction. The eyes widen, the jaw drops, and then there is the knowing nod. Yes, for us the St. Matthew really, unquestionably, has the power to reach that deep into one's soul.

But Barbara's response was different. Her eyes did widen, her jaw dropped, but with all the other musicians the effect would last for maybe ten seconds at most. Barbara seemed frozen. Nearly a minute went by, and her eyes began to mist over. Concerned, I leaned forward and asked, "Barbara, are you okay?"

It still took a few moments before she could speak.

Finally, she also leaned in and said, "Andrew, my husband David was the tenor soloist on that recording. He sang the role of the Evangelist."

The world doesn't get much smaller than that. We were both stunned. It took both of us some time to recover. But we did, and quickly made a plan. I offered to give David a private concert. Barbara loved the idea, and thought she should assemble a small group of David's friends, all musicians, to join in.

Three days later, late on a Thursday afternoon, we met in a corner of the ornate lobby of the Mary Manning Walsh Home on York Avenue at Seventy-second Street. I played a thirty-minute concert for David and Barbara and their friends—a composer, a conductor, a cellist, a music professor, all of them now retired, and a younger friend my age, a record producer. David was in a wheelchair, and had trouble speaking, but listening to the music clearly gave him great pleasure.

As I neared the end of the program, I told them I would finish with some Bach. But first, I said, I had a little story to tell.

I recited that same nutshell of the story I'd told Barbara a few nights before. When I said, "The music in the iPod was Bach's *St. Matthew Passion*, the 1962 recording conducted by Leonard Bernstein," David's face suddenly transformed. His eyes were looking at me but I knew they were seeing past me. He was seeing and remembering, and feeling something that only he could know. I waited a few moments and then said,

"David, thank you for saving my life."

He was speechless. He continued looking silently at me but he was far away.

That moment passed. We could see he was exhausted. Barbara got up, we all said quiet goodbyes, and she wheeled him back to his room.

That was the last live performance of music that David Lloyd ever heard.

One evening, a few weeks after he died, Barbara and I were walking down Broadway—we live nearby. I'd always wondered if David had ever said anything to her about the concert and story.

She grew silent, stopped, and turned to me. "Yes, Andrew, he did, just once—that night, in fact. As we were getting him back into bed, he put his hand on my arm, looked up with a twinkle in his eye and a slight grin, and said, 'I should have sent him a bill!'" Barbara and I stood on the corner of Broadway and Ninety-ninth Street and we must have laughed, tears in our eyes, for a full five minutes.

At the end of the very first day I played music in the SICU, on Wednesday, January 20, 2010, I was making my way past the Nurses' Station to go home. Stanley Nimark, a respiratory therapist, came over to thank me for the music. He then said, "The most help you'll ever be to the staff is during a Code Blue. The music will help keep us calm." I've never forgotten his words.

Not long ago, I walked into the SICU just minutes after a patient, a Code Blue, had been rushed into Bed 9. One of the doctors and a physician's assistant saw me and they told me to unpack and get to the bedside ASAP. I had been considered by the doctors, nurses, and PAs to be part of their medical team for years now.

The patient had aspirated during surgery. He'd been in cardiac arrest in the OR, had been resuscitated there, and then arrested again on the way to the SICU. Nobody knew how many minutes he'd been gone, but all the signs were very bad.

I played for an hour as they worked on him. As was usual during a Code Blue, I imagined I was playing for dancers, helping to keep the medical team's movements fluid. I also made sure the music wasn't obviously happy or sad. I didn't want them to notice me—my role was to help their flow and keep them relaxed. There were about ten doctors and nurses around the bed, all with different responsibilities. I knew two of the surgeons at the bedside, great doctors I'd seen over the years. They understood and appreciated how helpful music was in a situation like this.

Finally, the most crucial work was done, and most of the team had moved on to other beds. I noticed that the patient's oxygenation level was just below a key marker. It was 79 percent. Blood-oxygen levels below 80 percent may compromise organ function, such as the brain and heart, and so this had been a great concern and still was. A nurse told me they'd been doing everything they could to bring it higher but it hadn't moved since the patient had arrived in the SICU. Since the space around the bed was now open, I moved in much closer and began playing

248 • WAKING THE SPIRIT

music conducive to deeper breathing—faster, more dynamic, and dramatic. Not specific music, but improvisations. I'd discovered early on that this made it easier for me to just concentrate on the rhythm. Fifteen minutes later, without letting up for a second in the music, the oxygenation level hit 81 percent.

Just then I saw Dr. Vladimir Rubinshteyn, the newly hired attending physician, third in command of the SICU, walking at a good clip from the other end of the unit, wearing his purple surgical scrubs. Originally from Moscow, he'd done his medical training at Temple University in Philadelphia, and a fellowship in surgical critical care at New York-Presbyterian/Weill Cornell Medical Center. He was already well liked by the staff. We'd recently met for the first time and had a good chat about music and medicine. He was very interested in learning more about it because he'd had very little experience with it in his training.

As he passed Bed 9, I asked him if he had a minute and he stopped and said, "Yes, but just a minute."

"Dr. Rubinshteyn, once everybody cleared out I pulled up close and played for this patient for the last fifteen minutes and his oxygenation level went up two points, and broke past eighty percent. It's easy to understand music's calming effect on heart rate and blood pressure, but I've seen this happen so many times with oxygenation, too, and I've always wondered how it works, what the underlying mechanism is. Do you know why it has that effect?"

Rubinshteyn got very serious, looked down, was clearly thinking hard, and then looked up, met my eyes and held them for a moment. Speaking slowly and carefully—his English is excellent but he has a strong Russian accent—he said, "I . . . have . . . no . . . idea."

He turned quickly and started to leave but, after walking about ten feet, he suddenly spun around with a pirouette worthy of a Bolshoi Ballet dancer, and with the absolutely perfect devilish grin that he was already famous for in our little place on the third floor, he said,

"Just keep playing!"

Afterword

By Marvin A. McMillen, M.D., FACS, MACP

Over the past thirty-two years, I have cared for about thirty thousand surgical intensive care unit patients in major teaching hospitals and medical schools in Buffalo, Minnesota, Brooklyn, New Haven, Chicago, the Bronx, Manhattan, and the Berkshires. Many of these patients have shared both their fears and insights with me. It seems that most of us experience a diagnosis of life-threatening illness as if it has never happened to anyone else. It's a paradox of our awareness that, as much a part of our lives as critical illness may be, we do not begin to comprehend its impact until it's upon us. Until it's up close and personal, and hits us as a profound, existential loneliness.

In 1979, I was training as a transplant surgeon when I learned I had polycystic kidney disease, an illness that would lead to kidney failure and dramatically alter and shorten my life. I was dumbstruck by the way my colleagues—at a progressive medical

school, a world leader in the study of kidney disease—were emotionally unavailable to me as I tried to understand the life consequences of this genetic illness that could be passed on to half
of my children and would likely kill me at about age fifty. Any
effort on my part to discuss my diagnosis and its implications was
met with discomfort and physical and emotional distancing.
Most of my associates were in their early thirties, and as they
continued to plan their lives and careers, I felt very isolated and
alone. The professors weren't much better—they were used to
lecturing in an auditorium, not facing an anxious junior colleague across their desk. Over the years, I have said it was as if I
had "gone over to the enemy." I had become a patient with a life-
altering illness who, one day, would become critically ill myself.

I have since spent my life and career moving back and forth,
from critical care doctor to critical care patient, and back again.
I have stared up at the ceiling from the bed in four different
intensive care units during a four-year period, hooked up to a
breathing machine and a kidney dialysis machine, hoping that
my fluid overload would be corrected, my breathing would improve, my potassium would decrease, and that I would leave
the unit alive with a bit more time and life to enjoy. And, each
time, a few weeks later, I have found myself as the doctor at the
bedside in the ICU, explaining how the ventilator and dialysis
machine work, and what the implications are of "shock" and "sepsis." I know that a hospital bed is not the place to reorder one's
priorities or think about what matters most in what might be
the last months of one's life. And a surgical intensive care unit
is about the worst place I can think of to come to terms with the
meaning of critical illness. The chrome, monitors, beeps, and

alarms turn a modern intensive care unit into the antithesis of the "healing environment." No patient sleeps for more than one hour at a time without being awakened for nursing procedures and vital signs checks. Flowers are banned. All the life cues to the real world are sacrificed to the needs of sterility and function. It's little surprise that most patients in an ICU have higher-than-normal blood pressure, heart rate, and so on—just due to the stress of being there.

How then can we best help a patient and family coming to grips with the reality of their illness, the recovery from their desperate situation, or the ritual of saying goodbye? As a child, I grew up near the grandeur of Niagara Falls, and as an adult I've found that my experiences as gardener, hiker, and fisherman in beautiful places affect how I process difficult information or disappointment. This idea of the healing environment is important for me—and for my patients. How to take the humbling shudder of Niagara's thunder, or the perfect early morning in a summer garden, or the sun setting at the head of my favorite trout stream and import that beauty and well-being into this ICU world of chrome and bandage, screens and machines, noise, worry, and fear? How to use it to help a patient and their family cope and survive? What are really the most powerful aspects and tools of the healing environment?

In the hospital administrative literature I have read here in the United States, "healing environment" is sometimes a catch-phrase for commercial hospital architecture and design. In the United Kingdom, a more broad definition has been embraced, one that includes horticulture therapy, art therapy, and music therapy as medical modalities. There, the King's Fund has become an important catalyst and crossroads for ideas about healing and environment. And a critical element of this effort is that it is very much centered on the needs of the individual patient.

The conductor Daniel Barenboim has said that live music has such emotional power over us because it is gone the moment after we encounter it—"Every note is a lifetime for itself." We listen to it; it disappears; and we long to hear it again. While I can stare at a Turner harborscape until I tire and then move on to the next in the knowledge that the first painting awaits my return, the chorale of Beethoven's Ninth is taken from me the moment it is performed. Music is processed in our brain differently than visual art—in the "old" brain, where blood pressure and heart rate are controlled. Rather than visual or cognitive input in the optical or temporal cortex flowing inward, music enters our brain adjacent to processes that are fundamental to our very existence. Music may have a power over us that visual art does not have, going back to our mothers singing to us while still in the womb.

Patients newly diagnosed with life-threatening and critical illness often experience dysphoria, a slide into deep depression. It seems as if a shade has come down over their perception of life, a filter has been placed on their thought and vision. The world looks different and experience comes in differently. After the statement, "Well, it's cancer, and it's inoperable," few patients process the information that comes next. The shock of the diagnosis acts like malware in a computer program—the computer has to be rebooted or reprogrammed to move forward.

Music has the power to help us reboot. For my generation, listening to recorded Peter, Paul and Mary, or James Taylor, or Edith Piaf might reconnect us to a time in our lives when all

AFTERWORD • 255

things seemed possible. And Beethoven's Ninth, "Rhapsody in Blue," or operatic pieces like *Nessun Dorma* connect us to the universe and the sublime. The musical "prescription" may be both common and varied for each of us: some music is appreciated nearly universally for its beauty, and some is associated with memories and experiences that enhance its personal impact. From this connection, we can all draw strength, perspective, and the resolution to face an illness and its consequences. For the last few years, I have advised my friends to include a playlist on their advance directives. I'm not joking.

Live music can be even more powerful than recorded music. Cabaret musicians, musician survivors of critical illness, and empathetic music therapists can take the power of therapeutic music a step further. Yehudi Menuhin created Live Music Now, a musician development and outreach program in the United Kingdom, to emphasize the connection between musician and audience. A concert musician up on the stage, floodlights in his face, demonstrates his craft, and takes in the appreciation and applause from an audience out in the darkness. However, a cabaret musician sits facing her audience, seeing their faces and expressions, and she performs and shares in a whole different way. It is a two-way relationship.

In 2004, my own odyssey as a dialysis patient with intermittent critical illness ended with the miracle of a kidney transplant, an anonymous gift from the family of a deceased donor. My transplant continues to function well and has given me eleven years of life quality and enjoyment I never expected to have.

Andrew Schulman and I share the bond of those who have endured great suffering and been granted more time to come back to the world with a new way of seeing. During our illnesses we both learned that music, art, and gardening were amazingly important and comforting in our pain and uncertainty. Fortunately, we both have the opportunity, in our professional lives, to try and improve the healing environment for others.

Andrew has taken his transformative experience of his altered perception after his own diagnosis, and the impact of his love of music at a critical point in his own recovery, and brought it back to the bedsides of his ICU listeners. His insight is not that he knows how *they* feel, but that he remembers how *he* felt when he was the patient in the bed. It is impossible to join the patient or family in their isolation and fear, but he introduces them to the brotherhood of the desperately ill who understand they can no longer pretend to be immortal. He works with the family and patient to find the "prescription" of that music most meaningful to help the patient in their journey. In the process, he has taught us about a powerful tool we in the medical world should employ more widely in our therapeutic efforts.

A new medical specialty, palliative care, emphasizes patient-centered treatment both for recovering patients and during end-of-life care. It may seem surprising that a patient's physical and emotional care has not always been the top priority in modern medicine, but patients have long had to be treated in a way that works best for the health care industry. In recent years, both patients and doctors have begun to ask for—and to see—positive changes in this area. For example, medical staff and patients increasingly appreciate that the physical and emotional costs of major surgery and/or chemotherapy may exceed the benefits to the patient. The price of survival alone may be too great from the standpoint of a patient's enjoyment of life. So then the emphasis shifts to living the rest of one's life well, refocusing, and sharing in the time one has left rather than being subjected to every last medical maneuver. There's a turning toward humanism.

Hopefully, in the worlds of surviving critical illness and in end-of-life care, the "musical prescription" will increasingly be part of the therapeutic plan. And for both musician survivors of desperate illness as well as empathetic music therapists, there will hopefully continue to be development of this powerful tool in the armamentarium of "the healing environment"—the musician at the ICU bedside.

Notes

Prologue

6   *There is a clinical research study under way* Beth Israel Medical Center, "Effects of an Integrative Music Therapy Program on the Perception of Noise in the SICU: A Patient, Caregiver, and Physician/Nursing Environmental Study," ClinicalTrials.gov (Bethesda, M.D.: National Library of Medicine, 2000), accessed July 12, 2015, https://clinicaltrials.gov/ct2/show/record/NCT02269527.

7   *Dr. Sacks . . . has said* Oliver Sacks, *Musicophilia: Tales of Music and the Brain* (New York: Alfred A. Knopf, 2007).

7   *Dr. Joanne Loewy . . . led a landmark study* J. Loewy et al., "The Effects of Music Therapy on Vital Signs, Feeding, and Sleep in Premature Infants," *Pediatrics* 131, no. 5 (2013): 902–18.

7–8   *Dr. Ralph Spintge . . . has conducted studies* R. Spintge, "Clinical Use of Music in Operating Theaters," in R. A. R. MacDonald, G. Kreutz, and L. A. Mitchell, eds., *Music, Health and Wellbeing* (Oxford: Oxford University Press, 2012), 276–89.

8   *On August 13, 2015* P. Glasziou, "Music in Hospital," *The Lancet* 386, no. 10004 (August 2015): 1609–1610, accessed August 21,

2015, www.thelancet.com/journals/lancet/article/PIIS0140-6736 (15)60640-7/fulltext.

10 *I found this quote, within seconds, from neuromusicologist Dr. Arthur Harvey* Honolulu Star-Bulletin, April 29, 2004.

1. The Ultimate Reality

15 *of the approximately forty-nine thousand pancreatic cancer diagnoses every year* Cancer Facts and Statistics 2015, accessed July 12, 2015, www.cancer.org/research/cancerfactsstatistics/cancerfactsfig ures2015/.

4. Awakenings

57 *Cognitive scientists posit* Christie Aschwanden, "Where Do Thoughts Occur." *Discover Magazine.* May 20, 2013, accessed July 12, 2015, http://discovermagazine.com/2013/june/12-where-do -thoughts-occur.

5. Returning

65 *Two Beatles songs, two Bach preludes, and two Spanish pieces* "Here Comes the Sun," "In My Life," *First Cello Suite* Prelude, Little Prelude in D minor, "Recuerdos de la Alhambra," and "Anonymous." ("Anonymous" was the theme of the film *Forbidden Games,* one of the most recognizable guitar pieces of all time, and known worldwide simply as "Anonymous.")

67 *"Every day is alone in itself, whatever enjoyment I've had, and whatever sorrow I've had. . . . It's like waking from a dream."* B. Milner, "Memory and the Temporal Regions of the Brain," in K. H. Pribram and D. E. Broadbent, *Biology of Memory* (New York: Academic Press, 1970), 37.

68 *states that there is a time gradient in retrograde amnesia* Th. Ribot, *Les Maladies De La Memoire* (Paris: Librairie Germer Balliere, 1881).

70 *details the music therapy work she and her team have undertaken* Loewy et al., "The Effects of Music Therapy."

6. Goin' Home

80 *using operating rooms, anesthesia rooms, and surgical waiting rooms wired for music* Spintge, "Clinical Use of Music in Operating The-

atres," 276–86. Spintge's results also show other clinical benefits of specific music interventions, including increase in pain threshold and pain tolerance and reduction of pre- and postsurgery medication.

81 *music offers a real clinical benefit to patients suffering from depression* Anna Maratos et al., "Music Therapy for Depression," *Cochrane Collection [EBSCO]*, 2008, accessed July 13, 2015.

86 *The American Music Therapy Association (AMTA) states that music therapists* "What Do Music Therapists Do?" musictherapy.org, accessed July 13, 2015, http://www.musictherapy.org/faq/#39.

7. Everything Vibrates

91 *I knew the Bible story of David* 1 Samuel 16:14–23.

93 *Greek society held the number seven as sacred* Jamie James, *The Music of the Spheres: Music, Science, and the Natural Order of the Universe* (New York: Grove, 1993).

97 *a big impetus to getting it started as a profession began during World War I* William B. Davis, Kate E. Gfeller, and Michael Thaut, *An Introduction to Music Therapy: Theory and Practice* (Boston: McGraw-Hill, 1999).

98 *from the Roosevelt era set up to provide employment in the aftermath of the Great Depression* Davis et al., *An Introduction to Music Therapy.*

8. Alice Blue Gown

106 *music is built into the human cells, especially brain cells, from the hour of conception* Galina Mindlin, Don DuRousseau, and Joseph Cardillo, *Your Playlist Can Change Your Life: 10 Proven Ways Your Favorite Music Can Revolutionize Your Health, Memory, Organization, Alertness, and More* (Naperville, IL: Source Books, 2012), 10.

119 *research paper on diagnosis of vegetative states appeared in* Science in 2006 Adrian M. Owen and Martin R. Coleman, "Detecting Awareness in the Vegetative State," *Annals of the New York Academy of Sciences* 1129, no. 1 (2008): 130–38, http://onlinelibrary .wiley.com/doi/10.1196/annals.1417.018/full.

119 *incapable of demonstrating their consciousness through standard clinical assessments* Mo Costandi, "Detecting Covert Consciousness in the Vegetative State," *The Guardian*, September 2, 2011, accessed

July 14, 2015, www.theguardian.com/science/neurophilosophy/2011/sep/02/detecting-covert-consciousness-vegetative-state.

121 *music is strongly associated with the brain's reward system* Valorie N. Salimpoor et al., "Anatomically Distinct Dopamine Release during Anticipation and Experience of Peak Emotion to Music," *Nature Neuroscience* 14, no. 2 (2011): 257–62, www.nature.com/nrn/journal/v15/n3/full/nrn3666.html.

10. Getting to the Other Side of the Rainbow

149 *"as if in amber, in the music, and people can regain a sense of identity"* Oliver Sacks, YouTube video, 3:44, "Musicophilia—Alzheimer's/The Power of Music," September 22, 2008, posted by Random House, accessed July 15, 2015, www.youtube.com/watch?v=M.D.YplKQ4JBc.

11. Through the Gate

159 *part of a paper by Memorial Sloan Kettering Cancer Center music therapist Lucanne Magill Bailey* Lucanne Magill Bailey, "Music Therapy in Pain Management," *Journal of Pain and Symptom Management* 1, no. 1, (1986) 25–28.

160 *introduced their gate control theory of pain* R. Melzack and P. D. Wall, "Pain Mechanisms: A New Theory," *Science* 150, no. 3699 (1965): 971–78.

160 *research done during and following World War II by Dr. Henry Beecher* Henry K. Beecher, "Pain in Men Wounded in Battle," *Annals of Surgery* 123, no. 1 (1946): 96–105.

161 *"The soldiers were not unhappy about their wounds"* "Pain Linked to Attitudes," *The Milwaukee Journal*, December 20, 1956, p. 16, accessed July 20, 2015.

161 *As Melzack later said* Ronald Melzack, YouTube video, 10:26, "Ronald Melzack: Pain Pioneer," October 6, 2010, posted by McGill University, accessed July 23, 2015, www.youtube.com/watch?v=KRFanGlnvlc.

162 *One in particular is especially illuminating* Andrew Rossetti and Bernardo Canga, chap. 16 in *Music and Medicine: Integrative Models in the Treatment of Pain* (New York: Satchnote, 2013).

12. Just Don't Kill the Patient

173 As research psychologist Gary Klein puts it Bill Breen, "What's Your Intuition?" FastCompany, August 31, 2000, accessed July 21, 2015, www.fastcompany.com/40456/whats-your-intuition

178 Mozart once wrote about his own music in a letter to his father Emily Anderson, The Letters of Mozart and His Family, vol. 3 (London: Macmillan, 1938), 1242.

178 Ständchen is a great example of music as Henry Wadsworth Longfellow, "Ancient Spanish Ballads," in Outre-mer: A Pilgrimage Beyond the Sea, vol. 2 (New York: Harper & Bros., 1835), 4.

181 studied brain activity during fMRI brain scans of people listening to songs D. Sammler et al., "The Relationship of Lyrics and Tunes in the Processing of Unfamiliar Songs: A Functional Magnetic Resonance Adaptation Study," Journal of Neuroscience 30, no. 10 (2010): 3572–78.

186 "The aim and final reason of all music" Hans T. David, Arthur Mendel, and Christoph Wolf, The New Bach Reader: A Life of Johann Sebastian Bach in Letters and Documents (New York: W. W. Norton, 1998), 17.

13. The Music of Poetry, the Poetry of Music

203 respond to music that produces "shivers down the spine"—specifically, a brain region associated with reward Adam Zemen et al., "By Heart an FMRI Study of Brain Activation by Poetry and Prose," Journal of Consciousness Studies 20 (2013): 132–58, www.ingentaconnect.com/content/imp/jcs/2013/00000020/f0020009/art00008.

14. Steppin' Out with My Baby

208 being resuscitated or hearing specific beeps from medical machines Sam Parnia, "AWARE—Awareness during Resuscitation—A Prospective Study," Resuscitation 85, no. 12 (2014): 1799–805.

Resources

I. Music and Medicine Resources by
Barbara L. Wheeler, Ph.D., MT-BC

(Barbara L. Wheeler initiated the music therapy program at the University of Louisville in 2000, retiring in 2011. She is professor emerita at Montclair State University and currently affiliated with Molloy College and the State University of New York–New Paltz. She is a past president of the American Music Therapy Association.)

As a music therapist, I was happy to read Andrew's book. I have worked as a music therapist in clinical settings and as a university professor for more than forty-five years and have lectured and presented around the world. Throughout all of this, I have observed and heard of many wonderful things that have happened to people in their experiences with music and music therapy. Those that Andrew reports are among the most re-markable.

I am delighted to share some resources to supplement An-drew's narrative about his amazing journey. I will point to some that I think are good and try to give some perspective of what is useful and what might be better left alone. Many of these are available through the Internet, although some will need to be accessed through libraries or purchased. I have divided them into three areas: music therapy, music and medicine, and music for one's own use, although there is some crossover as not all re-sources fall into one clear category.

Music Therapy

Music therapy is the use of music with a client (one of the words that is used to refer to the participant in the therapy process) by a music therapist. Music therapists undergo extensive training, including supervised clinical experience, so not just any use of music qualifies as music therapy (as Andrew reiterated in this book). I caution you to be aware that only people who are Board Certified Music Therapists (in the United States) or have another music therapy credential (in other countries) are qualified music therapists. Other people use music in various ways—and many of them do good work—but should not call themselves music therapists. Music therapy is generally aimed toward clinical goals, intended to help the person receiving it to function better or become healthier.

Books

There are many good music therapy books; I will recommend just a few general books here and refer readers to some publishers whose Web sites include dozens of other books. These five provide good overviews:

Azoulay, Ronit, and Joanne V. Loewy, eds. *Music, The Breath and Health: Advances in Integrative Music Therapy.* New York: Satchnote Press, 2009.

Bunt, Leslie, and Brynjulf Stige. *Music Therapy: An Art Beyond Words.* 2nd ed. London: Routledge, 2014.

Davis, William B., Kate E. Gfeller, and Michael H. Thaut. *An Introduction to Music Therapy: Theory and Practice.* 3rd ed. Silver Spring, MD: American Music Therapy Association, 2008.

Mondanaro, John, and Gabriel Sara, eds. *Integrative Models in the Treatment of Pain.* New York: Satchnote Press, 2013.

Wheeler, Barbara L., ed. *Music Therapy Handbook.* New York: Guilford Press, 2015.

Many other excellent music therapy books are available, including some by publishers that specialize in music therapy publications. Here is a list of these publishers and a brief description of each:

Barcelona Publishers publishes exclusively music therapy books: barcelonapublishers.com.

Jessica Kingsley Publishers has a large collection of arts therapy

publications including many music therapy books: www
.jkp.com/usa/products?audience_codes=19&cat=107.

The Louis Armstrong Center for Music and Medicine at
Mount Sinai Beth Israel in New York City has published many books that have come from the symposia
on various aspects of medical music therapy they have
hosted for many years: www.wehealny.org/services/bi
_musictherapy/pubs.html.

The American Music Therapy Association (AMTA), the
professional association for music therapists in the United
States, publishes many music therapy books: Go to www
.musictherapy.org and click Bookstore > Visit the Bookstore.

There are many other excellent music therapy books that
are not published by one of these specialized publishers.
A good place to find some of these publications is the
West Music Web site: www.westmusic.com/s/music
-therapy-books-and-materials.

Other Information on Music Therapy

There are many music therapy journals, including those published by the professional associations from various countries:

Voices: A World Forum for Music Therapy (www.voices.no) is
an online, free journal. It provides an international perspective on music therapy and is highly recommended.

Information on music therapy in countries around the world
is available through Web sites for most associations (e.g.,
www.bamt.org—British Association for Music Therapy).

The World Federation of Music is the best source for information about music therapy worldwide, and its Web site contains a range of useful information: www.musictherapy world.net/.

Here are some Web sites that will lead you to valuable information about music therapy (descriptions are from the organizations' Web sites):

The Louis and Lucille Armstrong Music Therapy Program at Mount Sinai Beth Israel in New York City provides regular music therapy sessions for patients in the neonatal intensive care unit, pediatrics, family medicine, maternity, oncology, respiratory step-down, intensive care units, Peter Krueger Clinic, orthopedics, hospice, pain medicine, and palliative care. The LACMM is directed by Dr. Joanne Loewy, DA, MT-BC, LCAT. www.musicandmedicine.org.

The Institute for Music and Neurologic Function's groundbreaking and internationally recognized programs use music therapy to assist the "awakening and healing" of individuals with a wide range of neurological conditions, including strokes, trauma, dementia, Alzheimer's, and Parkinson's diseases. The IMNF is directed by Dr. Concetta M. Tomaino, DA, MT-BC, LCAT, with medical guidance by cofounder and honorary board member, Dr. Oliver Sacks, until his death in 2015. http:// musictherapy.imnf.org.

The American Music Therapy Association (AMTA) has many resources available. Its mission is to advance public awareness of the benefits of music therapy and increase access to quality music therapy services in a rapidly changing world. www.musictherapy.org.

Music and Medicine

Music and medicine is the use of music by medical professionals. It often employs recorded music but may utilize live music. I would like to mention two excellent resources:

The International Association for Music & Medicine (IAMM) brings together arts medicine, music performance, performance arts medicine, music psychology, medical humanities, ethnomusicology, music cognition, music neurology, music therapy, music in hospitals, infant stimulation, and music medicine, promoting an integrative perspective to applied music in health care. IAMM sponsors a journal, *Music and Medicine,* and an international conference every two years. www.iammonline.com/.

As described on the journal's Web site (www.iammonline .com), "*Music and Medicine* is an integrative forum for clinical practice and research related to music interventions and applications of clinical music strategies in medicine. Each peer-reviewed issue offers original articles, case studies, commentaries, and interviews from clinical medicine, the neurosciences, behavioral sciences, nursing, and social work that translate music, music psychology, music cognition, music neurology, and music therapy into scientifically valid clinical applications." Abstracts of all articles are available in a number of languages, although full articles are only available with a subscription.

Personal Uses of Music for Health

Many, if not most, of us use music for our personal well-being and enjoyment. However, sometimes people wish for more guidance in how to do this. I am going to recommend some resources, focusing on those written by or recommended by music therapists, because they have a great deal of training and experience in using music for health and go through a rigorous process in order to become board certified (or achieve a professional designation specific to the country in which they practice). I am sharing some that I have found to be valuable.

Books

Buchanan, Jennifer. *Tune In: A Music Therapy Approach to Life. Use Music Intentionally to Curb Stress, Boost Morale, and Restore Health.* Austin, TX: Hugo House Publishers, 2012.

Hanser, Suzanne B., and Susan E. Mandel. *Manage Your Stress & Pain through Music.* Boston: Berklee Press, 2010.

Katsh, Shelley, and Carol Merle-Fishman. *The Music Within You.* New Braunfels, TX: Barcelona Publishers, 1998.

Stevens, Christine. *Music Medicine: The Science and Spirit of Healing Yourself with Sound.* Louisville, CO: Sounds True, 2012.

Although none of these is specifically about music and medicine, they are landmark books about music and the brain, and they connect well to several of the patient stories in *Waking the Spirit:*

Levitin, Daniel J. *This Is Your Brain on Music: The Science of a Human Obsession.* New York: Penguin Books, 2007.

Sacks, Oliver. *Musicophilia: Tales of Music and the Brain.* New York: Alfred A. Knopf, 2008; and *The Man Who Mistook His Wife for a Hat: And Other Clinical Tales.* New York: Touchstone, 1998.

Web Sites and Blogs

A number of Web sites and blogs written by music therapists present information related to music therapy and using music to promote health for the general public. An overview of blogs—focused on music therapy—is at http://musictherapyactivities .wikia.com/wiki/Music_Therapy_Blogs.

I hope you find some of these resources useful as you explore ways to use music to enrich your own lives and the lives of those who are important to you.

II. More Resources by Andrew Schulman, Guitarist

Johann Sebastian Bach

As Wendy has said, the indisputable hero of this book is Johann Sebastian Bach. Here are a few of the recordings of his music that have meant the most to me personally, some books that I've found to be invaluable for insights into the man, a documentary film about Bach and his music told through the performances and words of some of the best musicians of our time, and a Web site with loads of great links:

Recordings

The Musical Offering. BWV 1079. Nikolaus Harnoncourt: Concentus Musicus Wien, Elektra/WEA, 1970.

The *St. Matthew Passion.* Leonard Bernstein, Collegiate Chorale, New York Philharmonic. Soloists: Adele Addison, William Wildermann, David Lloyd, Charles Bressler, Donaldson Bell, and Betty Allen. Columbia Masterworks Records, 1962, rereleased on Sony Masterworks, 1999.

The Well-Tempered Clavier, Book I. BWV 846–869. Mieczyslaw Horszowski, piano. Vanguard Classics, 1979–80.

Books

David, Hans T., and Arthur Mendel, eds. *The New Bach Reader: A Life of Johann Sebastian Bach in Letters and Documents.* Revised and expanded by Christoph Wolff. New York: W. W. Norton, 1998.

Wolff, Christoph. *Johann Sebastian Bach: The Learned Musician.* New York: W. W. Norton, 2001.

A Film

Bach and Friends, directed and produced by Michael Lawrence: www.mlfilms.com/productions/bach_project.

A Web Site

This Web site will take you all over cyberspace to learn more about J. S. Bach. The painting of Bach seen on the home page is the same one I saw at my first classical guitar lesson when I was a little boy: www.jsbach.org.

Further Listening

A few weeks after I returned home from the hospital after my surgery and the medical crisis that ensued, I went to see my primary care physician who, at that time, was nearing retirement age. I told him about the music during my coma. On my next visit, he told me he had prepared a special iPod with *his* favorite music and written instructions that it be used should he be hospitalized and critically ill.

When asked to recommend the best medical music, my answer is, as I've said throughout the book, only you can answer that. The relatively small investment of time to prepare yourself for a medical emergency with your favorite music is time well spent. It could speed your recovery and possibly even save your life. Choosing a hospital with an established music therapy program, whenever possible, is wise, too.

Music and the Brain

The Internet is filled with evidence of the growing interest in music and the brain. The following Web sites are excellent places to find more information on all aspects of the subject:

Institute for Music & Brain Science (www.brainmusic.org): Mark Jude Tramo, M.D., Ph.D., is the director and a founding member of its executive board. He teaches at the David Geffen School of Medicine at UCLA and the UCLA Herb Alpert School of Music. The institute's online library is one of the largest repositories of its kind: www.brainmusic.org/EducationalActivities.html.

Music for Health Services (www.musicforhealthservices .com) and **Healing Music** (www.healingmusic.org): Neuromusicologist Arthur W. Harvey, M.M., DMA, has two Web sites. He can be contacted directly through Music for Health Services for more information, including about the course he taught at the School of Medicine at the University of Louisville in Kentucky described in chapter 12. Resources about the healing power of music can be found through his other site, Healing Music.

Z Lab (www.zlab.mcgill.ca) and **Brams: International Laboratory for Brain, Music, and Sound Research** (www.brams.org/en): Both run by Robert J. Zatorre, Ph.D., a cognitive neuroscientist and researcher at the internationally renowned Montreal Neurological Institute, a McGill University research and teaching institute. His principal areas of research focus on two complex and characteristically human abilities: speech and music.

McGill University's Laboratory for Music Perception, Cognition and Expertise (http://daniellevitin.com /levitinlab/LabWebsite):. Run by Daniel Levitin, Ph.D., author of the bestselling book *This Is Your Brain on Music*.

Brain Resource Center of New York (www.brainresource center.com): Kamran Fallahpour, Ph.D., who explains a lot of the neuroscience in the patient stories in this book, is a clinical psychologist, neuroscientist, and director of the Brain Resource Center. His clinical practice and research activities increasingly involve the use of music and sound.

Music and the Mind

Dr. Richard Kogan is a concert pianist, psychiatrist, and the artistic director of the Weill Cornell Music and Medicine Program. He lectures on the influence of psychological factors and mental illness on the creative work of composers.

> "Mindscape: Richard Kogan, M.D., on the Trauma of Beethoven's Deafness." YouTube video, 12:57. Posted by the Menninger Clinic on May 28, 2015, https://www.youtube.com/watch?v=HycW7YO-3e0.
>
> Kogan, Richard. "Richard Kogan, M.D., on Chopin." YouTube video, 7:10. Posted by "ats343" on May 25, 2015, https://www.youtube.com/watch?v=3XmmXKqx-Sc.

Dr. Kogan gives lecture/performances all over the world: www.apbspeakers.com/speaker/richard-kogan.

Music and the Military

I have always been interested in military history and its connection to music. Musicians through the millennia have led soldiers into battle, and now music is helping to heal the physical and mental wounds of active military personnel, veterans, and their families nationwide through many different music therapy programs. Here are some examples of places where programs are in place, as well as some specific programs:

Davis-Monthan Air Force Base, Tucson

Resounding Joy Inc., San Diego, a nonprofit organization whose mission is to promote social, emotional, physical, and spiritual well-being through music, sponsors many music therapy programs for military personnel including:

Balboa Wounded Athlete Program, Naval Medical Center
Overcoming Adversity and Stress Injury Support (OASIS) program at Naval Base Point Loma in San Diego
Semper Sound Music Therapy Program at Camp Pendleton
Traumatic Brain Injury Group, Naval Medical Center, San Diego
National Intrepid Center of Excellence (NICoE), Bethesda
Walter Reed National Military Medical Center, Bethesda
Institute for Therapy through the Arts (ITA), Music Institute of Chicago, Oaktree Program, Chicago

The American Music Therapy Association sponsored a white paper in 2014: "Music Therapy and Military Populations: A Status Report and Recommendations on Music Therapy Treatment, Programs, Research, and Practice Policy." www.musictherapy.org/research/music_therapy_and_military_populations/.

Coma Dreams

Dr. Steven Ellman, Ph.D., a psychologist-psychoanalyst, is a leading authority on dreams and explained to me the impact my coma dreams had on my decision to return to the SICU as a musician. He is the coauthor/editor of a highly regarded book about dreaming: Steven J. Ellman and John S. Antrobus, *The Mind in Sleep: Psychology and Psychophysiology* (1991). Learn more about Dr. Ellman here: http://postdocpsychoanalytic.as .nyu.edu/object/faculty.steven.ellman.

Music Biography

Deena Rosenberg and Ernie Harburg contributed greatly to this book. They are both authors and their books, mentioned in chapter 10, are:

Meyerson, Harold, and Ernie Harburg. *Who Put the Rainbow in The Wizard of Oz? Yip Harburg, Lyricist.* Ann Arbor: University of Michigan Press, 1993, www.press.umich.edu /14211/who_put_the_rainbow_in_the_wizard_of_oz.

Rosenberg, Deena Ruth. *Fascinating Rhythm: The Collaboration of George and Ira Gershwin.* Ann Arbor: University of Michigan Press, 1999, www.press.umich.edu/8490 /fascinating_rhythm.

The Composer

Thierry Lancino is the composer of *Requiem*, mentioned in chapter 12, and many other works: www.lancino.org.

Music and Poetry

John Peters, the poet in chapter 13, has had his work published by http://westbeth.org/wordpress/artists/literary-artists/. His *Marijuana Poem*, with music by pianist George Winston, was videotaped four months before I played for him in the SICU: https://www.youtube.com/watch?v=9oX0Y2qoo7c.

Lindsey Tate

My editor, Lindsey, is both an author and an editor. Prior to her work on *Waking the Spirit* she did extensive research on the brain for two other books: *Shouting in the Dark* about blind artist John

Bramblitt and *Mind Reader* about mentalist Lior Suchard. She also writes children's books. www.LindseyTate.com.

Andrew Schulman

For more information about *Waking the Spirit*, including how to get my recordings of music referred to in the book, and updates about continuing research and new developments in music and medicine discussed in the book, go to: www.abacaproductions .com.

The story of *Waking the Spirit* is told in *Andrew & Wendy*, a thirty-minute documentary film by Josh Aronson, with commentary by Dr. Marvin McMillen, Dr. Martin Karpeh Jr., and Dr. Joanne Loewy: http://aronsonfilms.com/aw-info.html.

This three-minute news segment by WNBC-TV News, "Soothing Sounds in the SICU," won a NY Emmy and 1st Prize in the NPPA (National Press Photographers Association's) Best in Photojournalism series: http://player.vimeo.com/video /21132008.

BBC Radio 4's "Soul Music" is a series about music with a powerful emotional impact. The final one explored Bach's *St. Matthew Passion* and included my story: www.bbc.co.uk/programmes /p0195k95.

The Abaca String Band: When I'm not playing in the SICU I play concerts and make recordings with the string quintet I founded in 1991: www.abacaproductions.com/stringband.html.

A Note on the Music

The music on the book's jacket is the opening melody of Bach's *St. Matthew Passion*. The music that appears under the chapter titles is represented here in full. This Sarabande, which I played the day I returned home from the hospital after my stay as a patient, begins with the same melody as the final chorus of the *St. Matthew Passion*.

Sarabande

BWV 997

J. S. Bach
Arranged for 8-string guitar
by Andrew Schulman

Acknowledgments

This book emerged from a journal I started on my first day as a musician in the SICU. My friend, Beth Mead, was my first reader of that journal and made many excellent suggestions, and she and her husband, Lyndon Laminack, my longtime guitarist/ mandolin player/doctor buddy, were the first to encourage me to take it to the next step.

Jody Hotchkiss of Hotchkiss and Associates, a friend of Wendy's and a longtime fan of her singing, got the ball rolling after reading the first sample chapters, came up with the title, and has been a friend of the book and to me every step of the way.

He connected me to my wonderful book agent, Marly Rusoff, who inspired me in our first phone call to reach higher than I ever thought I could, and to her partner, Mihai Radulescu, who has the sound of the guitar forever in his heart. Marly never gave up on me, even in the roughest of waters. She asked Ayesha Pande to edit the book proposal, which she did expertly while encouraging me greatly. As a result, the proposal found a home, *allegro vivace.*

My publisher at Picador, Stephen Morrison, had the keen insight to shape this book into something more than a guitar player telling stories of the power of music to heal. It was his vision to reach out to the highly accomplished experts in the field of music and medicine who have contributed so much to this book, adding ballast to the stories I told. P. J. Horoszko, first as assistant to the publisher and then as associate editor, has been enormously helpful in this process from start to finish, and is a fellow guitarist to boot. Henry Sene Yee, who designed a fantastic book jacket with a clue in the music notation about going into and coming out of a coma, James Meader, Kolt Beringer, Steven Seighman, Susannah Noel, Elizabeth Catalano, Marlena Brown, and Shannon Donnelly—Picador, a superb team.

My editor, Lindsey Tate, was a godsend, the perfect book doctor when this project found itself in the Book Intensive Care Unit. Her Theo and our Paco and Phoebe started playing together in the Eighty-seventh Street dog run in Riverside Park in Manhattan; we met, shared a vision, and every single day of work with her has been filled with the joy of learning and creating. Without Lindsey's brilliant mind and skill I could never have woven together the incredible range of human experience in the SICU that I've been part of since July 16, 2009.

The doctors: There would be no book or afterword, and no Andrew, without Dr. Marvin McMillen, director of the SICU when I was a patient and during my first two years as a musician there. Dr. Martin Karpeh Jr., my surgeon, didn't let me play the guitar during my operation (I offered to, really), but as chairman

of surgery at Beth Israel he enthusiastically encouraged and supported my work as a critical care musician. Dr. Mason Mandy
assisted in the surgery, and without his quick thinking on the
mad dash of a ride from the OR to the SICU, I never would have
survived. Dr. Simon Eiref said yes to the music during my coma,
thereby giving the ultimate hook to the story, and he was a
comforting presence to Wendy and me in the days after I awoke.
Dr. Asaf Gave, director of the Mount Sinai Beth Israel SICU
since 2012, has taught me a great deal about the medical part of
being a medical musician. Dr. Arif Chaudhry, Dr. Sarah "Promenade" Edwards, and many other surgery residents have helped
me in countless ways. Dr. Vladimir Rubinshteyn gave me a great
gift for the book: a perfect ending! Dr. Michael Grossbard recommended Dr. Karpeh to us. Dr. Gallina Glinik was there for
Wendy and me that first weekend. Dr. James Jeng joined the
SICU team just as the book was completed—he plays the guitar
and piano, and knows how important medical music is. Dr. William Inabnet, now chairman of surgery, loves jazz and also
understands the value of medical music. Dr. Avram "Coop"
Cooperman gave me key pancreas advice and taught me to swim
when I was six years old.

Special thanks to Dr. Jason Bratcher, who has watched over
my pancreas like a hawk ever since my surgery so I can—I hope—
keep playing in the SICU until the day I die . . . again.

The physician's assistants: Barbara Gerbier, first to arrive at
Bed 11 when I was wheeled in; Nathan Boucher, chief PA when
I was a patient; and our current chief, Scott Gould. Ezra Gillego,
who helped so much with the book. The PAs are indispensable.

The nurses, my heroes: Those who took care of me when I

was a patient and helped me when I returned as a musician—Margot LeStrange, Will Burga, Rosievic Hamilton, Madelene Castro, Mildred Daroy, Flora Balasa, Faye Cayabyab, Pilar Baker, Richard Spatafora, Annette Shields, Teresa Bernandino-Duran, Leyla Farraj, Elizabeth Okyere-Bour, Agatha Penny, Ulrica Maynard, Karen Gottlieb, and Marina Yuditskaya, among so many others. Listening to their gentle laughter and camaraderie and learning from them, and from the patient care attendants, too, was a big part of why I returned to the SICU and stayed.

Thanks to *all* the different specialists in the SICU, especially to respiratory therapists Jeffrey Vogel and Stanley Nimark but many others, as well.

Dr. Kamran Fallahpour explained much of the neuroscience in the patient stories in the book, and his sage wisdom guided me many times over the past year. He performed the qEEG scan that I underwent and also arranged for the brain MRI done at the Gruss Magnetic Resonance Research Center. Thanks to Dr. Michael Lipton and his assistant, Malka Zughaft, for making that happen.

Dr. Stephan Quentzel, medical director of the Armstrong Center, and Dr. Ronald Kaplan, director of Acute Pain Service at Mount Sinai Beth Israel, were very generous with their time, elaborating on how music can inhibit pain.

Dr. Richard Kogan shared his fascinating insights about the role of psychological factors on the creative work of composers.

Dr. Steven Ellman explained much about what coma dreams really are. Thanks to Dr. Carolyn Ellman, who urged me to watch *The Story of the Weeping Camel*, a deeply moving film about how powerful music really is.

Dr. Mark Mankoff taught me so much about what makes us

who we are, a most valuable asset when you're playing for criti-cally ill patients and writing about it.

Dr. Mark Jude Tramo shared his vast knowledge of music and the brain with me. Mark's assistant, Sean Mooney, was most helpful in steering me to the right information.

The lawyers! Henry Kaufman checked everything with a fine-tooth comb and made great suggestions for the text, and my lawyer and friend, Ola Ogunye, also did a careful reading and gave much encouragement.

The world of music and medicine: Dr. Joanne Loewy, direc-tor of the Louis Armstrong Center for Music and Medicine, has been my host from the beginning and has made many valuable contributions to this book.

John Mondanaro, the clinical director of the Louis Arm-strong Center for Music and Medicine, also made many valuable contributions to this book.

Dr. Bryan Hunter and Dr. Barbara Wheeler were very gener-ous in sharing their vast knowledge about the history and scope of music therapy.

Al Bumanis and Judy Simpson of the American Music Ther-apy Association were a great help with key information about music therapy and also gave encouragement for this book.

Dr. Oliver Sacks and Kate Edgar, Dr. Sacks's longtime col-laborator and editor, very kindly suggested I contact Dr. Connie Tomaino, Dr. Sacks's cofounder of the Institute for Music and Neurologic Function, for help in understanding how my brain healed so I could play from memory again.

Connie and I were young once, students at Stony Brook where she was the first person to tell me about music healing. It was amazing to have her be, thirty-five years later, the first to confirm how music had healed me.

Dr. Arthur Harvey shared his knowledge about why Bach is best when it comes to balancing the brain; we had several long and fascinating telephone conversations.

Steve Schneider, musician and music therapist, shared many insights about critical care music.

Thanks to Dianne Wawrzusin of the American Music Therapy Association and Sharon Moorman of CC Thomas Publisher for help in securing permissions for the history of medical music quotes.

Many thanks to the JM Kaplan Fund and Richard Kaplan and Edwina Sandys for a grant to Dr. Marvin McMillen so we can develop teaching programs for medical musicians. And to the D'Addario Foundation, John D'Addario Jr., and Jim and Janet D'Addario for many years of support and encouragement.

Many thanks to my friend and neighbor, composer Thierry Lancino, who shared his thoughts about his magnificent *Requiem*; to my friend and fellow survivor, guitarist John Clary, who told me about Plotinus and the "ultimate reality"; and to my friends, musicians extraordinaire Barbara Wilson Lloyd and David Lloyd, for creating the moment that allowed things to come full circle.

Filmmaker Josh Aronson, who told the story in his documentary film *Andrew & Wendy*, a gem, and who took the photo of me for the book.

The guitar crew: Guitar makers—Darren Hippner, whose guitars have helped soothe and heal hundreds of critically ill patients; Gary Lee, who is designing a new guitar for me especially for use in the SICU; and John Gilbert, who taught me so much about intonation. The guitarists who shared their thoughts about what makes the guitar such an ideal healing instrument: Ben Verdery, Liona Boyd, Jerry Willard, Frederic Hand, Paul Herzman, Barry Pollack, Perry Beekman, Andrew Rossetti, and Marcia Feldman. Fan-Chia Tao, the director of research and development and string designer for D'Addario & Company, hit the nail on the head about why the guitar is an ideal medical instrument.

Most of the extraordinary experiences I've had in my life have happened in the past five years in the SICU. A most special thank-you to the patients and family members who were so kind to give me permission to tell their stories and use their real names in the book.

In order as they appear:

Deena Rosenberg and Ernie Harburg. Gordon Taylor. John Peters. Bob Harper and Emily and Matt Gilfus. Elliott Bernerd, Trudie Malawer, and David Reynolds. I have stayed in touch with all of them, and so many others whose lives I've been privileged to be a part of in trying times. I've gotten much more than I've given in every instance.

My friends who graciously helped a first-time author with expert advice:

Albert and Edith Fried, Kristin Lancino, Liel Liebovitz, Kris Kline, Susan Elliott, Katie Gilden, and Thomas Vinciguerra.

To friends, colleagues, and family, to whom I am forever grateful, who have helped in so many ways:

Robert Crim and Suzanne Schwartz, the Awner family, Nancy Ford and Keith Charles, Dr. Carrie Barron and Dr. Alton Barron, Victoria Elliot, Suzanne Shepherd, Victor Sachse, Dan Grayson, Alison Jukes, Jill Caruth, the Baer family, the Guber family, Ruth and Michael French, Art and Manijeh Bruegge-man, Dr. Philip Brotman and Judy Kellersberger, Conrad Leven-son, Sarah White, the Allison family, Mayra and Jon Pardo, Steve Yeager, Roth Wilkovsky, Louis Schenkel, Carol Rubiano, Jim Mandler, Kenneth Brown, Mikael Elsila, Nicki Nolan, Suzanne Bardsley, Nina Sanderson, Andrea Valencia, the Saivetz-Romero-Snyder families, and my sisters, Roni Gilden and Kathi Jacob, and their families.

Most special thanks: to my father, Sydney, whose love of music was a beacon of light as far back as I can remember, and my mother, Sylvia, who always wanted me to be a doctor and is now immensely proud that her son the guitarist helps heal those who need it most.

And finally, to my wife, Wendy, the love of my life, who was the driving force for this book from the beginning, did all the history research, and has saved my life in many ways more times than I can remember.

In loving memory: our Dolly (2002–2014) and Paco (2004–2015). Now keeping the tradition going: Little Phoebe (b. 2014). Music has the power to heal, but nobody loves you like your dog.

ABOUT THE AUTHOR

ANDREW SCHULMAN is the resident musician in the Surgical Intensive Care Unit at Mount Sinai Beth Israel hospital in New York City. He is the founder and artistic director of the Abaca String Band, which has performed throughout the United States. He is also a solo guitarist and has appeared at Carnegie Hall, the Royal Albert Hall in London, the Improv Comedy Club, and the White House. He lives in New York City with his wife, Wendy.